I leaned over close
to the bedroom mirror
and prayed that
it was deceiving me.

I ran to look
in the bathroom mirror.

It was true.
The other mirror
hadn't lied at all.

My hair *was* navy blue.

To: Derek with love
G-ma & G-pa J.
1984
Easter

We're in the Army Now!

IMELDIA MORRIS ELLER

LIVING BOOKS
Tyndale House
Publishers, Inc.
Wheaton, Illinois

First Printing, May 1982

Library of Congress Catalog Card Number 81-85928
ISBN 0-8423-7862-6
Copyright © 1982 by Imeldia Morris Eller
Printed in the United States of America

Dedicated to
the real sergeant in command

Donald Tilford Morris

WO-◼︎- 120th ARCOM

A special salute to all the other troopers

Commander W. Frank Morris, Jr., U.S. Navy

Sharron Morris Ratchford

John Stanley Morris

Susan Morris Orsini

and to

Mama

Special love and thanks
to my husband, Henry
and my son, Chris
for their unfailing love and support
and to my mother and mother-in-law
who have stood behind me and my family.

Fondest thanks
to Bobby Martin Morris
Juanita Morris Hoffman
and Carolyn Morris Hargett
who know more tales
about the Rainbow Army Gang
than anybody
and still love them
at least one-and-a-half times
more than anybody!

Warmest appreciation
to our good friends
George Shinn and C. J. "Jenk" Jenkins
for their encouragement throughout
the completion of this book
and to all the dear and wonderful friends
who've wondered for so long,
When are we going to see that book?

And finally, sincere thanks
to my manuscript editor, Vicki T. deVries
and to all the other encouraging friends
at Tyndale House.

CONTENTS

ONE
The Enemy

THERE's probably nothing worse than being called an orphan, unless it's really being one. My older brother Hank and I could stand being thought of as one, but neither of us could bear having our younger sisters and brother—Elizabeth, eleven; Lillian, barely six; and Jake, nine—suddenly being declared orphans too.

It was the social worker who informed Hank and me that we'd all become "wards of the county." Her words shocked and humiliated us. We were speechless when she told us that we'd all soon be placed in temporary homes.

"She's not putting me into any home!" I screamed when she left. I couldn't imagine our home, where noise and love abounded, standing cold and devoid of children's voices and laughter. "She's not putting any of us into one. I'll fight anyone who comes here and tries. Who

The stranger who came to our house

told her about us, anyway?" I asked, turning to Hank.

"Some well-meaning people, I suppose, Melanie," Hank said with a faraway look. His usual expression was a warm, wide grin that almost wrapped around his head, but that day everything had changed. Our whole lives had changed in the twinkling of an eye. It promised to be the test of Job.

"You mean 'do-gooders.' Well, it's none of their business! I hate them all," I said crying. "Let's run away, Hank, please," I begged.

"We can't run away, Melanie. We have

to stay here and fight—somehow. Besides, there's no place we can run to, and we have to stay in school."

"School. I hate school too, Hank! I don't ever want to go to school another day in my life. I just want to disappear and never be heard from again!"

"Now stop all that, Melanie! We've got to figure out how we can all stay together. That's the important thing."

"If they take us away, we can't stay together. Who wants five kids?" I stormed. "Nobody, not a single living soul. We'll all be separated, Hank. I know we will."

"No, we won't," Hank said. "Now I have a good plan. I'm almost sixteen, and you're fourteen, Melanie. We can run things here until. . . ."

"Until what?" I sobbed. "Until they come to take us? That might be tomorrow, and you know they're coming, Hank. The social lady said so, because it's the law, and she said we were all underage. You heard her."

"I know," Hank said, "but there's one of us who isn't underage anymore."

"You mean Dan?" I asked, my eyes wide like saucers. "But he's in the army and won't be home for another year. Besides, I didn't think you wanted to worry him with all the things going on here."

"I didn't, but that was before I realized we weren't considered old enough to run the show, even though we know we can. Anyway, he's going to find out. Besides, he *should* know. He's one of us. He's our brother!"

"But you know how Dan worries," I said.

"Yes, I know, Melanie, but Dan's twenty-one now. He's going to find out sooner or later, and he'll be more upset if he finds out later."

"But what good will it do for him to know? He can't do anything across the ocean," I said. "Besides, you know he can't just leave the army and come home, just like that."

"I know," Hank said more thoughtful than ever, "but if the right people know that he has two brothers and three sisters who are underage and homeless, maybe he can come home to stay."

Hank's last words set my alarm off again. "Don't say that!" I shrieked. "We have a home if people will just let us keep it!"

"I know, Melanie," Hank answered, "but what I said is the reality of it all—it's the way the rest of the world sees it."

It wasn't the way I saw it, and I decided then and there that *reality was extremely overrated.* For as long as I've lived, I've never forgotten the conclusion I drew that day: sometimes, reality is unfair to people, especially when they can't control it or are not old enough to do so.

Hank, trying to be encouraging, said in a very positive manner, "Maybe we won't have to leave home at all. If things move fast enough, why, Dan might just be on the next plane home. Who knows? But my plan is going to work, Melanie. Mark my word—it's going to work."

"Hank!" I yelled. "You think every situation will turn out rosey. Don't you understand that we're up against the whole world? That's a pretty big enemy."

"Not the whole world, just a small group, but since they have the upper hand, we'll have to win them to our side," Hank said thoughtfully. "Just let me handle it, but please cooperate, Melanie, and don't be such a rebel."

"Nobody's going to see our side, Hank. If we compromise, we're licked, and you know it," I cried.

"You act like it's hopeless unless we turn this house into a fortress with live artillery sticking out of every window and door," Hank replied.

"I can think of nothing good that's happened in the past three years, and you still believe in miracles! Well, I don't believe in your plan, Hank. I don't believe in anything or anybody anymore!"

I stomped away, bitter, hurt, and angry at the whole world. My mind raced back over the past three years to the time when it had all started. It had all begun when Daddy lost everything he had, except for us and Mama. There were eight of us then.

Daddy had seen it all coming. He said, "The little man doesn't have a chance anymore, and it's too late for a man of my age to start over." When the giant supermarkets opened their doors, Daddy closed the doors of his little Community Grocery Store forever. That was the day Daddy started dying.

I'll never forget those long lonely days

Daddy's Community Store

Daddy spent in his little store before the
end came. People came in for only a loaf
of bread and some milk or some cigarettes
and snuff. Daddy sat all day studying his
big, worn Bible, which he propped on a
Coke crate. Then leaning way over it from
a wooden chair, he'd read and study
through glasses tilted on the end of his
nose.

Daddy aged from fifty to a hundred in a
week's time, it seems, and within the year
he was dead. "A heart attack," the coroner
said when he came to our house that
Sunday morning. But I couldn't accept it.
Daddy died from a broken heart.

Soon after that, Dan was drafted into
the army. He never got over Daddy's
death. Mama tried to hold things together,
but it all became too much for her.

Everything went from bad to worse. Mama was sick all the time. She didn't have much strength left and kept getting weaker. Pretty soon she couldn't get out of bed. Then she stopped eating and finally stopped talking.

We'd seen Daddy die. We couldn't watch Mama die, too. That was when Hank called the family doctor to our house. Mama wouldn't let us call him before. When he came, he was very distraught that Mama had not let us call him sooner. Sometimes Mama was as stubborn as her children could be.

The doctor took one look at her and told Hank he'd done the right thing by calling him. Mama's state of complete mental and physical exhaustion had gone too far, and she needed a long rest, but the local hospital was not equipped to treat Mama's condition. It was after she went away to the state hospital near the mountains that the social worker showed up out of nowhere with that awful news which, to me, brought the end of the world.

Part of Hank's plan worked and part of it didn't. An appeal was made through many caring people, even some who didn't know us, to bring our brother home. The Red Cross worked as hard as it could, but there was a lot of red tape involved, which we were told would take a long time to work out.

We still had to leave home, be separated, and live with other families for a time, but that is another story within itself. All the

Home—the place where noise and love abounded

way, I put up a desperate fight and beat
my fists against the walls, almost putting
holes in them. I refused to cooperate or
listen to anybody in any way. One of the
younger children told someone not to mind
me. "Melanie doesn't know what she's
doing because we've never seen her act so
ugly before." The other children accepted
everything very peacefully, while the whole
thing brought out the worst in me. I
worked myself into such a tizzy that I
wound up with symptoms which could not
be diagnosed.

My truce with the whole situation came only after I'd worn myself out completely, struggling until the victory of Dan's homecoming was seen on the horizon. And that is where this story begins—the day Dan came home and put our family back together again. We were finally all home again to stay, except for Mama.

TWO
The Homecoming

HANK was in charge on that memorable
morning when the five of us children
returned home again and were reunited as
a family. The house seemed noisier than
ever before, with all of us chattering at
once and hugging each other. Hank
wanted everything to appear as though
nothing had changed by the time Dan got
there. It didn't take long for the house to
look very lived in. Hank ran around
making sure everything still worked and
even had the phone reconnected. It started
ringing almost immediately. I guess
everybody knew Dan was coming home.
Thank heaven for that. Now, maybe some
people would stop thinking of us as "those
poor children," and shaking their heads
over it all.

The first curious phone caller was the
one the majority of us dreaded the most—
Miz Alexandria, the wealthy widow. She

First caller

spent her winters in our part of the
country and the short summer months at
her "other" home somewhere up in New
England. Jake once asked her if that was
in the United States. Now Jake knew very
well where New England is and got just
what he deserved from Miz Alexandria—a
geography lesson.

I don't know why Miz Alexandria was
interested in us. Maybe she was anxious to
know which one of us was going to "break

bad" or turn hoodlum first—Jake or me. It could have been that she just wanted to see how people lived on the other side of the tracks. She should have spent the night with us. That would have cured her for good, with all the trains passing through, every two hours of the night.

Miz Alexandria wasn't just curious—she was plain nosey. She'd been around long enough to know everything about every skeleton in every closet and attic in town, especially the ones that still had some meat on their bones. It was no wonder that when people saw her coming, they ran the other way, referring to her all the while as Miz Buzy Body, Got Rocks, Miz Buff Often, the Gold Digger, Ole Goody Two-Shoes, the Mouth of the South, and some I can't mention.

Elizabeth, like Dan, could see straight through people—clear to the other side. According to Elizabeth, Miz Alexandria wanted more than anything to be the "cat's meow." You'd think she'd know better than to throw her weight around when all she had was skin and bones beneath all the fur and the glitter. Everyone could see past all that.

Miz Alexandria wore fur even in May and August. (No one saw her the two months in between.) Jake thought she might be a bit chilly year round, so he once offered her some fatback to put oil in her system, to fatten her up, and to grease those poor stiff joints of hers. Miz Alexandria didn't know what fatback was. Jake said later he might have known that someone who ate snails and chocolate-covered ants wouldn't know good food when she saw it. Miz Alexandria didn't know what she was missing in a big, fat butter biscuit with sourwood honey dripping off of it!

Hank once made some very noble gestures on Miz Alexandria's behalf, but they didn't get past the kitchen sink at our house. He said, "Maybe Miz Alexandria is like she is because she's always had everything and because she's an only begotten child."

"So was Jesus!" Lillian exclaimed. "He was the Lord's only begotten child and was even a king and could have had the whole world, but he didn't turn out like Miz Alexandria!"

"And a little child shall lead them," Hank remarked in Lillian's direction, then turned to the rest of us. "Well, then, maybe we ought to pray for the poor old soul."

Elizabeth quickly responded without apology, "I can't bring myself to mention Miz Alexandria's name in the same sentence with anything that is heavenly."

And so it seems that Hank was the only one at our house who had continued patience and compassion for someone who really had no excuse being a troublemaker 365 days out of the year. He did once admit though that there were just two small things about Miz Alexandria that were irksome to him: her dangling earbobs and cateye spec' chains. But he never held it against her for wearing them or her fourteen layers of flame red nail polish!

No one knew how to handle Miz Alexandria any better than Hank. He had too much charm for just one person, and he could turn it on with Miz Alexandria. When she was the first caller the day we children were reunited, Hank started right off with it.

"Hello, Miz Alexandria," Hank drawled politely. "I'm so glad you called. Yes, Ma'am, we all came home this morning. Oh, really, Miz Alexandria? I'm sorry you had trouble getting through, but we do have thirteen families on our party line. Yes, Ma'am, thirteen. The best time to get the line on this end is when a train is passing through. Nobody wants the line then," Hank laughed. "You can't even hear yourself think, much less talk. Oh, we're all doing just fine. Everybody around here is fine as frog's hair, but how are you getting on these days, Miz? . . . Oh, I'm sorry to hear that. If there's anything I can do, just. . . ."

I knew that Miz Alexandria was going on about her bad back again and Hank would listen to it for the next twenty minutes or so, as if Miz Alexandria were the only human being ever to be born with a back, and a bad one at that.

One thing Hank never did in front of Miz Alexandria was put on airs, but he could be very dramatic. Hank's conversation continued, "We're trying to get everything perfect for Dan's homecoming, so I better run now and. . . . Oh, Mama? Mama's doing just fine. . . . Doctor says she'll be home in a week or two. Yes, it is

"The best time to get the line on this end is when a train is passing through."

wonderful. Why, I know Mama will be glad to see you, too, Miz Alexandria. Oh, thank you. Yes, Ma'am, we'll take real good care of things. Yes, Ma'am, thank you for calling, and you take good care of that bad back, now. Good-bye, Miz Alexandria."

Hank had bent Miz Alexandria's ear with "one big tall tale" about Mama coming home. There wasn't a word of truth in it.

"You told Miz 'A' a fib, Hank! A great big one. All those things you said about Mama coming home! You know they aren't true. Why did you say, 'Mama's coming home in a week or two,' when you know very well she isn't?"

"Because I like the sound of it," Hank said with one of his faraway gazes. "Besides, how do we know she's not? She might."

"That's just it—we don't know," I said. "That's why it's a fib."

"Just a little white one. It won't do any harm, and you can call it a fib if you want to, but I call it 'something to hope for,'" Hank said.

"Well, you told it to the wrong person. Now, everybody around is going to start asking why our Mama's not home yet."

"Well, we have two weeks to think up something to say," Hank answered. "Oh, I hope Miz Alexandria's somewhere in New England by then!"

"Me, too," I said. "Well, if people ask me any questions, I'm going to say, 'Ask Hank. He's the one who knows everything.' No, I couldn't be that mean. Maybe we could look in the Bible for an answer to all the questions that might come up. Remember when you once opened it up and then looked down and read the first thing you saw, just knowing in your heart it would be the exact answer you were looking for? And you read: *Judas went out and hanged himself.*"

"Yeah, that was the day I found out that you have to *search* the Bible for answers, but that story really happened to someone else. I just used it on all of you to get a good point across. And don't worry. I'll think of something to say!"

"You know, I don't mind *anybody* asking us about Mama, except Miz Alexandria. She blows everything up to be so much worse than it really is."

"I'm glad you finally decided, Melanie, that things are never as bad as you think they are!"

"But Miz Alexandria just loves going around saying things like, 'Tut-tut-tut, those poor dear children. Heaven knows what's going to happen to them with their Mama gone and all. Ah shorely do hope they don't all *go to the bad.* That would be sooo tragic.' And I can just imagine what she says about Mama," I continued mournfully. "Oh, I wish you hadn't told such a big whopper, if you had to tell one!"

"Oh, it's not so big," Hank responded confidently. "There you go again thinking things are bigger than they really are. There's just one more thing, and I want you to hold on to this, Melanie, *forever,* if you can. You might need it someday. Just remember that the Lord's idea of two weeks may not be the same as yours and mine, nor as Miz Alexandria's either."

I supposed Hank's attitude was right. Somehow, he always knew just what was right for us, even if the rest of the world might think it was wrong. He kept everything so altogether in his head and never once forgot where he put it!

Hank went back to the business of inspecting everything in the house, including Jake, Elizabeth, Lillian, and me.

"Jake, tuck your shirttail in," Hank said. "Mercy, you could use a session with the barber. Getting you there is going to be harder than standing on my head for three days. Guess I'll have to handcuff you, tie you up, and haul you there. Hey, what's that flopping out under your chin?"

Jake looked down. "I don't know. What does it look like?"

"Looks like the label of your undershirt. You've got that undershirt on backwards! Go turn it around. Miz Alexandria's liable to come by and want to read your label. And I'm sure it'd be the wrong one! Now, go on and change it, but you'd better head for the bathroom this time. You need to wash your ears again too. And don't forget to tuck that shirttail in either!" Hank yelled after Jake. "Lillian, who tied that sash for you?"

"Melanie tied it," Lillian beamed.

"Well, the bow is crooked," Hank stated. "Come here and let me tie it."

Hank yelled into the bedroom. "Melanie, remember the way Mama taught us to tie bows? You stand in front of the person and lean over their shoulder to tie a straight bow in the back. Works every time if you tie it upside down! Think you can remember that, now?"

"Yes, Hank," I answered, rushing into the room. "I just forgot this time."

"Melanie," Jake whispered to me. "You better start remembering to put the milk

26

"The correct way to tie a bow—upside down!"

and butter in the icebox, too, with all the other cold stuff, instead of under the cabinet with the pots and pans and the pork 'n beans. Dan will have a fit if you do that when he gets home."

"I know it, Jake. I'll remember," I promised.

"Ummm, Melanie," Hank said. "Do you think you could stretch that hemline down a notch? Your slip is showing a tad."

"But, Hank!" I exclaimed. "I've already let the hem down as far as it will go!"

"What Melanie needs is elastic hemlines, so she can jerk 'em down, or else have Elizabeth let 'em down for her, so they will at least be even for once," Jake said humorously.

"What about that pretty dark blue dress you used to have, Melanie—the one with all the polka dots on it?" Hank asked. "Why can't you wear *that* dress?"

"Because *she* is wearing it," I said, pointing to Elizabeth, who was just coming into the room. "I outgrew that dress two years ago. You know that Elizabeth wears my hand-me-downs and that Lillian wears hers."

Hank turned to Elizabeth. "Why, that polka-dot dress does fit you! Looks good on you, too. I believe you're going to be every bit of six feet tall, just like Mama!"

"But it would be so nice to have a dress that was all my own, right from the start. I'll have one someday, when I can make my own," Elizabeth sighed.

"I'm sure you will," Hank said. "You already have a good start. How many other eleven-year-olds can crochet, knit, embroider, make quilt squares, and darn socks?"

Elizabeth was also the only eleven-year-old that we knew of who was going on twenty-two. She and Hank and Dan were wise beyond their years. I don't know where the rest of us were when all that wisdom was given out—behind the door, I guess.

"Elizabeth has nimble fingers," Jake said. "What can you do, Melanie?"

"Well, I can cook," I said meekly.

"I hope you know more about it than you did last time Mama let you bake a cake. The whole thing exploded in the oven. You could smell that thing for a week," Jake said.

"At least it didn't smell like your jokes," I said.

"That's enough," Hank said, warming up to give us several sermons he had prepared for us before Dan's arrival. Both Dan and Hank were very good on sermons, and had no idea how well they could preach. Both were long-winded when they got on their soapbox, much like Grandpa Harris, who had preached all day, more than once in his life.

According to Hank, there were going to be quite a few changes made around our house by way of attitudes. First of all, there would be no more complaining about what we didn't have and more talk about what we *did* have instead—which was a lot more than some folks. Second of all, there would be no more negative talk around the house. For example, if a peanut butter jar were sitting around filled to the halfway mark, we were to say, "Why, this peanut-butter jar is *half full!*" instead of "This peanut-butter jar is *half empty,*" which is what we would normally be apt to say.

We gave a weak, but promising, response to Hank's sermon, which he said he'd never bring up again.

And the last thing we were to remember from then on was that somebody somewhere loved Miz Alexandria, even if it was only the good Lord and her mother. We were to make an effort, no matter how meager it was, to find something good in her, too.

Even though Hank was totally aware of Miz Alexandria's love for certain brands, there was to be no more branding or labeling of her at our house as there had been: no more Ole Money Bags, Motor Mouth, Miz Magnolia Blossom, The Six O'Clock News, Town Tightwad, The City Slicker, and Miz Uppity-Uppity. I had the feeling nobody was going to mention Miz Alexandria's name around our house for a long, long time!

"When Miz Alexandria is talking about us, she is giving someone else a rest, and it is also free advertisement for us," Hank said.

"We'd rather pay for it!" we responded, adding we didn't like being the headlines when Miz Alexandria was the newscaster.

Hank went on to say something about how when negative words hit the air, they stayed in the atmosphere for a hundred years, or it could have been a million years. I don't remember.

"Say, Dan'll be here any minute!" Hank exclaimed. "Let me look at you all. Everybody smile. You look so bright and colorful."

"Like fireworks on the Fourth of July," Jake added.

"But at least we're all back together again," Lillian said.

"You're right, Lil, and that's a lot to be

thankful for," Hank said. "We owe all that to Dan, which reminds me. Let's practice up on our manners. You know how much Dan likes order."

"We know how to act," said Jake.

"Well, don't everybody go rushing out the door at once or talking all at the same time," Hank said.

"Why not?" Jake asked. "That's what we always do when somebody comes, 'specially if we haven't seen 'em in a long time. We did it last time Dan came home."

"I know, but that was some time ago. I just don't want to see any of the star-spangled personalities around here making Dan feel shell-shocked or dizzy. I want him to know we've all grown up *some*, at least."

"We have?" Jake asked.

"Well, I have," Hank said.

"Since when?" Jake wanted to know.

Since I had all those nightmares about graduating from a school for wayward boys—that's since when."

"That was a nightmare!" Elizabeth gasped. "What did you do in your dream that was so bad that you were sent to a place like that?"

"Nothing," said Hank. "I just kept dreaming that nobody understood me and that nobody knew what slot I was supposed to go in."

"What does that mean?" asked Lillian, who had been much quieter than usual all morning.

"It means they didn't know exactly where they should put me, Lillian, so I ended up in the wrong place."

Hank turned to Jake.

"Now, Jake, I started with all those bad dreams right after I learned that you had broken all those lamps playing basketball in the living room of the home where you were staying."

"But, Hank, I didn't mean to do it. I was lonesome and bored. I wish I could undo the whole thing."

"I wish I could undo a lot of the things that've happened to us, but I can't. The good thing is that they're all behind us now. We've got to start from right here. And now!" Hank said. "So let's forget the past and think about tomorrow. OK, everybody?"

"OK," we all said together.

"Just remember that everything happens for a reason, even though we don't understand why, and that we learn from our experiences whether they be good ones or bad ones," Hank said.

"We'll remember," Lillian said, speaking for all of us.

"Good. Now, back to our manners," Hank said. "All right, everybody, act civilized, not like a bunch of heathens, morons, or monkeys. Try to be calm, and Jake, no tomfoolery, or Dan's liable to jerk a knot in you, and you know he can, too. And. . . ."

Hank stopped. A strange dark car was pulling slowly into our driveway. It was important looking, with writing on the side. It made me think of the kind that either leads a parade or a funeral.

Everyone was still. It was just like the quiet after a storm when the sun breaks through all the clouds, and you aren't afraid anymore. We held our breaths and you could almost hear every heart beating. Then Lillian broke the silence.

"It's Dan! Oh, everybody, Dan's home! . . ."

Everybody forgot about grown-up, civilized manners. We flew out the door and down the steps, acting like the uncivilized heathens, morons, and monkeys Hank had forbidden us to imitate. And Hank was the biggest monkey of the bunch!

THREE
Getting Drafted

DAN looked like a dignified general, as Lillian and Jake bombarded him with questions.

"Whad'ya bring us, Dan?"

"Are you still in the army?"

"One thing at a time," Dan answered. "Yep, I'm still in the army, but I'm in the reserves now, and I have a full-time job with them, too."

He pulled a water canteen from his bag and handed it to Jake.

"Wow!" said Jake. "Now I can play war-and-camp-out."

"Where's my present?" Lillian asked softly.

"It's on its way," Dan answered.

"Tell me what it is," she pleaded.

"It's a surprise," Dan answered.

"Please give me a hint," she begged.

"If I do that, Lil, you'll know what it is," Dan said.

Lillian had a way with Dan just as she had with all of us. She could get to anyone's heart, including Jake's. By this time she was on Dan's lap.

He whispered some clues into her ear, and she leaped from his lap, with her top-secret information safely locked away.

"Tell us," Jake said, trying to con her.

"I can't do that," she answered. "Then it won't be a surprise."

"Shucks, Lil! You're so stubborn," Jake scorned.

Dan looked out the kitchen window. "I see Mr. Reavis still has his outhouse and junkyard."

"Yeah, but he's got more junk than ever," Jake added. "Never sells any of it—just keeps on collectin' it."

"Who'd want corroded old refrigerators, rusted bed springs, 500 flat tires, or any of those other broken-down old things?" Elizabeth snorted.

"Some people might," Lillian said defensively. "I see lots of cars slowing down to get a look at everything as they pass by."

"It'd take a year to see everythin' that's over there," Jake said, "countin' all the critters he's got, too."

"You'd think Mr. Reavis was a junk-collecting farmer instead of a house painter, with all those chickens, bird dogs, horses, and billy goats running loose with the junk," Elizabeth said.

"But the goats eat up the grass, and Mr. Reavis don't never have to mow," Lillian said.

"The only time I ever saw Mrs. Reavis mad was the day one of those billy goats was about to eat a shirt right off her clothesline," Hank laughed. "Boy, was she mad! Bless her heart, she chased that goat with a broomstick."

Oh, Dan!" Lillian exclaimed. "You should see Mr. Reavis's tattoos. They're left over from the army, when he was in the war. Do you have any tattoos, Dan?"

"No, Lil," Dan replied. "No battle wounds, not a one, except for this here place on my finger from tryin' to open a tin can with an army knife."

"Mr. Reavis knows lots of war stories and always keeps a good joke up his sleeve," Jake said.

"Yes, and he carries you high with all his war stories, too, Jake. . . . He fought in the most raging battles, you know. Talks about his army days all the time," I said, turning to Dan.

"Now there ain't nothin' wrong with the army," Dan said. "Made a man outta me."

"Are you home from the army for good, Dan, to take care of us?" Lillian asked.

"That's right, Lil. You don't ever have to leave home again. I'm head of this house now, and you all got to mind me. You hear?"

"Yes, sir!" Jake said, saluting.

"That's not the way the army salutes, Jake. I'll teach you the right way," Dan said.

"Will you teach me all you learned in the army?" Jake asked eagerly.

"As much as I can," Dan answered. "I

The Rainbow Army
Gang standing at
attention

don't know of no other way to raise you except the way the army would! So from now on, you might as well consider yourselves in the army!"

"The real honest-to-gosh army!" Jake exclaimed.

"No, silly," Elizabeth said. "Just Dan's army. Do we girls have to be in the army too, Dan?"

"Yep. And it'll be purt near the real thing, Elizabeth," Dan replied. "'Cause it works, and that's all I can tell you."

"Are we—like—drafted?" Jake asked.

"Yep. Right into basic training. It'll start early in the morning, so be ready, all a you," Dan said. "I'm tired out now—think I'll go lie down awhile."

Dan was serious about teaching us army ways. I could tell, because he had that certain frown on his face that said so. There was no way of getting the army out of Dan now. It was stuck in him for good, and soon it would be stuck in all of us.

"Dan sure likes the army, don't he?" Jake said.

"Yes, but he was a lot like that even before he got into the army," Elizabeth said. "I remember."

"You're right, Liz. I'd say the army hadn't changed Dan one iota," Hank said.

"He hasn't lost one bit of his Southern accent," said Elizabeth.

"He may even have a worser one," Lillian added.

"That proves one thing," Hank said. "You can take the boy out of the country, but you can't take the country out of the boy!"

"Looks to me like he's goin' bald 'round his forehead," Jake remarked.

"No, he isn't," said Hank. "He was born that way. I even think he was born with his glasses on. He's had 'em ever since I can remember. He's always had the same wrinkled nose that goes with his frown. They all go together with the horn-rims to keep 'em from falling off the tip of his nose."

"I think he was at least thirty when he was born," I said. "That should make him ancient by now."

"And smart, too," said Elizabeth. "Someone should write a book about Dan. His summers with Otis and Melvin would fill one book alone."

It was hard to imagine all of us growing up in the very same house and yet being so different. As a youngster Dan had spent his summers rollicking deep in the country with our rambunctious, yet easygoing cousins, Otis, Melvin, and Minnie Ruth, and their parents, Uncle Ollie and Aunt Isadora. We all envied Dan something fierce, because the next thing to being with Tom Sawyer and Huckleberry Finn was kicking up the dust with Otis and Melvin on their huge farm.

They all ran barefoot together in "Osh Gosh" overalls, through the cotton rows and the cornfields, rose at 4:00 A.M. to milk the cows, ate hoecakes and johnny-cakes made from scratch, went to corn shuckings, foot stomping fiddle-pickings, and grand all-day Fourth of July celebrations! Dan shared many adventures with Otis and Melvin, including their farm chores, their good horse sense mixed with "real" Southern manners, their church pew, and their turnabout sleeping at the foot of the bed.

The country folk practiced the philosophy that "happiness is homemade," just like Grandma's quilts and *real* hand-churned butter. They were the kind of people who have always stood as the backbone of our great land. Dan learned from Otis and Melvin the art of being "genuwine all the time," and how to have enough respect and humility to speak Southern *the right way.*

Jake was gathering those same fine arts from Dan, as if somehow they were becoming long forgotten treasures. Elizabeth thought Jake's "riches" could use some polishing now and then and suggested once that he refine himself a little, in case he got invited to the White House someday. Jake suggested that she "tune up her tacks" (tact) in case she got invited there.

"I know how to act!" Jake said, adding, "As far as I'm concerned, anything refined comes out of one of those refinery factories or off some assembly line where everything looks the same by the time it reaches the end a the line."

We just had to accept the fact that Jake and Dan were not about to change their stripes for anybody, dead or alive, even if they went around the world fourteen times and ended up living next door to the White House when they got back.

Elizabeth knew deep in her heart, just as the rest of us did, that Dan and Jake, like Otis and Melvin, would stand steadfast forever as the salt of the good earth. Anyway, we all got a nice sprinkling and flavoring of it daily from them both, just to remind us that some things should never be lost through the changing of times—like being "genuwine all the time" and "speaking Southern the right way."

We talked the rest of the day about being in the army. Hank made a big production of it all, calling our inspection line "Rainbow Row." He named us the "Rainbow Army Gang" because none of our uniforms matched. He gave us each a special color that matched our personalities.

Elizabeth said she'd rather join up with a bunch of gypsies because our new name was a bit mushy, farfetched, and flowery. Hank said emphatically, "So are we!" and continued the business of directing the show and casting colors.

Queenly Elizabeth was assigned royal blue because she so utterly deserved it. I complained that her blue dress used to be mine, but I still didn't get the royal color. Instead, I got the next thing to it—purple. Lillian's color was gold, since she was like sunshine. Jake got red—like rich red clay. Hank said Jake was a big, soft lump of it. Hank took the color orange because it was the brightest color in the sunset—and in the sunrise too and all during the day. We

Viewing the steeple

decided green should be Dan's color—army green.

Lillian said we looked like an Easter parade while Jake said we looked more like a bunch of Easter eggs, all dyed and decorated with plaids, stripes, polka dots, and flowers. Elizabeth said, "At least all our eggs are back in one basket."

With that good thought, I went to bed early our first night home. It was good to be back in the room I had shared with Lillian and Elizabeth. The bottom bunk bed felt good. I thought I heard whippoor-wills calling faraway and crickets chirping outside my window. Crickets meant good luck, especially if they came into the house. It was not quite the time of year for them, but my imagination was serving me well with favorite memories of home. The days were getting longer now, and signs of spring were on the way.

From my window I could see the steeple of the church that we attended every Sunday. It was where Daddy's funeral had been. The day had been hot. Organ music played as we filed into the church and filled the pew reserved for us. I looked at the gray and copper box in front of us. I couldn't believe my Daddy was inside it and that I'd never see his face again. My worst thought was that he was going to be put into the ground and covered up with dirt. It horrified me so that I couldn't bear to think about it without crying.

Dan had taken Daddy's death harder than anybody. He carried Daddy's Bible for weeks after the funeral and cried for days. The rest of us cried in our beds at night. When the lights were out at ten, all through the six-room house with its paper-thin walls could be heard the sounds of weeping. We all cried ourselves to sleep.

New and different feelings of our loss followed with each new day for many weeks after Daddy died. None of us talked about our feelings. My own feelings seemed insane. When the sadness went away, it was replaced with anger. I was angry at Daddy for dying and leaving us. I was also angry with God for taking him away. I didn't speak to God for a long time after that, either. I wanted to punish God. Even when I felt I'd punished him enough, I couldn't apologize for being mad at him. My angry feelings came back again when Mama went away.

My thoughts of death and dying were interrupted by Elizabeth and Lillian coming to bed. They must have thought I was asleep because they were so quiet. Being quiet was easy for Elizabeth, whose thoughts were often a mystery to me, but being quiet was hard for Lillian. The second week of school she had brought home a note from her teacher which said in big, bold letters: LILLIAN JUST CAN'T STOP TALKING!

In no time Lillian was on the bunk above me, saying her prayers which always took a long time. Lillian had great compassion for all living things, and she remembered them all in her prayers.

Just as I was about to doze, I heard a

little voice from above. "Melanie, are you asleep?"

"No, are you?" I asked.

"No. Did you know that Jake punched a boy out on the playground last week?"

"Really?" I said. "Jake's not much of a fighter. He'd rather count cows or chase girls with frogs. Are you sure it was Jake?"

"Yep, it was Jake all right. When the boy started crying, Jake said next time he'd really give him something to cry for."

"Next time *what?*" I asked yawning.

"Next time the boy said something about the hospital where Mama is."

My eyes popped wide open. "In that case, I don't blame Jake."

"I don't blame him much either. When Hank told us we should own our feelings, no matter how bad they might seem, Jake sure wasn't ashamed to claim his for Mama's sake, was he?"

"No, he sure aired them out, didn't he? I guess sometimes you have to be very brave to claim your feelings or else end up sick or depressed and never become the person you could really become."

"Melanie."

"Yes, Lil."

"Mama's just tired, isn't she?"

"That's right, Lil. Tired all over and she's taking a good long rest for it, too."

"I know," she answered. "I hope it wasn't us that tired her out so. I think it was a lot of things. I'd claim a long rest too after what Mama's been through! Jake said that Mama may have given out, but 'she ain't given up, and she ain't goin' to!'"

"That's right. Now go to sleep, honey," I said.

Lillian sighed, "Good night."

I gave her our standard good-night gesture from the bottom bunk: a little poke through the mattress with my toe.

I glanced one last time at the church steeple—the skinny pyramid which had so much courage to stand alone in the night. I wanted to be like the steeple. I was certainly thin enough, but I didn't have the courage yet. I was glad the view from my window was the steeple. It seemed to give me hope.

I thought once more of the view from Mama's kitchen window—the scenic view: Mr. Reavis's junkyard and outhouse sometimes referred to as the "backhouse." Honeysuckles flourished around it. They smelled so sweet on a summer's evening.

If it hadn't been for the outhouse, there would have been no honeysuckle vines. They clung to the sides of the gray, weathered building, which served as Mr. Reavis's refuge from the world. It was the first place he went to every morning and the last place he went to at night. There were rumors that Mr. Reavis kept a little brown jug there, but I never saw any proof of it.

I honestly liked Mr. Reavis, just as Lillian did. He let us play softball in his backyard. The outhouse served as first base, his clothesline post was second base, and his back-door steps were third

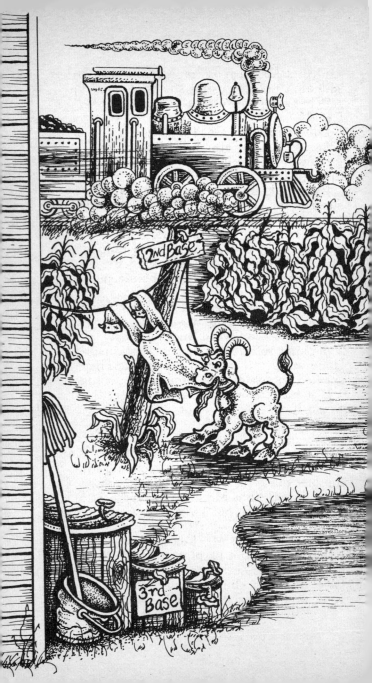

Mr. Reavis's refuge . . . and our softball
"field". . .

base. Third base always needed
repairing. The plank steps were forever
split and falling down. I never worried
about my foot getting stuck between the
planks, like everyone else. I seldom made
it past first base. I never was good at
softball, but I did get to smell the
honeysuckles now and then.

FOUR
Basic Training and S.O.P.

SIX o'clock arrived before the dawn's
early light and Sergeant Dan kept his
word. Basic training began with Dan
shouting into every bedroom his down-
home reveille call: "Rise and shine. Hit the
deck. Haul out on the double and move it,
move it, move it!" Dan combined army
talk with the language of the Navy, the
Marines, and the Air Force. All military
talk was the same to Dan.

The house began to rumble and shake.
An early morning train was approaching.
The railroad tracks were up a little
ridge just beyond our backyard so that
we had to look up at them when the
trains passed through. My bed started
to tremble and move across the floor, just
as everything quivered and moved to the
thunder of the trains. Teacups and
saucers rattled in the kitchen.

Passing trains were equal to minor earthquakes, and the way they soared above us was like living under a roller coaster. But we were used to the sounds of the trains—they were part of our lives. Across the tracks a rooster crowed. I often wondered whose rooster that was. I loved its song, sounding the dawning of a new day.

Everyone "hit the deck" and dashed for the bathroom. Dan stood at the door and put the "quaetus" on our stampede. No one spoke a word except for Dan. I arrived just in time to hear, "From now on, this here latrine is under S.O.P. That means 'Standin' Operatin' Procedure.'"

Dan rattled off the rules of S.O.P. I stood with my legs crossed and waited out the rules of S.O.P. I heard very little of what Dan said.

Waiting had never been an easy chore for me. My eyes didn't open until I'd bumped into at least three things or more. Getting to the bathroom was always the most important thing in the world. While I was waiting my turn, I'd usually droop like a rag doll until somebody would tap me and say, "Hey, Blondie, wake up! It's your turn now."

On the morning Dan introduced S.O.P., I was too sleepy to worry about those new rules. I wouldn't worry about them until they were reviewed again later. Besides, I was safe inside the bathroom. No one banged on the door or shouted, "Hurry up," while I was in there. I was the last one to fall in line for my turn!

As I left the bathroom, I could smell bacon cooking. I wandered into the kitchen and looked for Mama to be standing at the stove. It was Dan instead. I wasn't dreaming. Mama was truly gone.

"Mornin', Melanie," Dan said. "Crack some eggs and set the table, would you?"

That turned out to be a difficult mission for me so early in the morning. My fingers still wouldn't move, and I had no grip in them until I'd been up and moving about for at least an hour. I had trouble buttoning things and tying shoelaces or sashes for my younger sisters. It was an early morning handicap I tried to hide from my family since all my efforts during this time of day seemed to be the display of a scatterbrain. I fumbled to find the eggs and a bowl and managed to find the plates and some silverware. When I left the kitchen, the table was set and everyone was herding in, all dressed for breakfast.

I dressed quickly and returned just in time for Lillian's prayer. She loved saying the blessing, and it was always her very own, straight-from-the-heart, lengthy prayer. Each time you'd think she was about to say "Amen," she'd start back up again on something she'd forgotten to pray about. Finally, one morning when five stomachs all growled at once, Dan cut her blessings short. When he thought she'd given enough thanks, he shouted, "Amen," quick and loud, at a point he considered a good stopping place.

Lillian looked up startled. "But I'm not finished."

Dan commented in a firm tone, "That was a real nice prayer, Lillian. I'd like for you to save some of it for dinner and supper."

She smiled and agreed to do so.

Her prayers thereafter would be briefer in accordance with Dan's wishes, but they contained certain phrases indicating to Dan that his turn to pray was coming: "And now, dear Lord, before Dan says 'Amen,' please bless everybody, but especially Mama, and please let her come home soon."

We went over the rules of S.O.P. again after breakfast. Dan had another list of rules and regulations, duties and chores. The duties were equally distributed, and everyone had to make his or her own bunk so that you could bounce a coin on it. Dan demonstrated how that was done. "Bunks have got to be made as soon as you're out of them," he added.

Dan asked me to post the rules of S.O.P. on the bathroom door—just in case someone forgot them. I listed the rules as Dan had read them and drew cartoons of everyone lined up to get into the "latrine." A latrine duty chart was outside in the hall. That and the rules of S.O.P. were held up by Band-Aids until Dan brought home a super stickum tape guaranteed to last until doomsday!

Before the dawn's early light!

RULES OF S.O.P.

1. No more banging on the latrine door and hollering, "Hurry up," so you can get in quicker.
2. No more than three people of the same sex in the latrine at the same time. (You can hardly turn around in it as it is.)
3. Scrub tub clean after using it.
4. Hang all bathmats and towels to dry. No more mildew, understand?
5. No more soaking wet washcloths left around in the tub either. Wring 'em out and hang 'em up.
6. Keep all supplies put away where they belong. Everything goes somewhere and you know it!
7. Roll up toothpaste tube from the end so it don't look twisted, all beat up, and bent outta shape. (This prevents waste, too.)
8. Use towels more than once. (If possible!)
9. Throw dirty clothes in hamper, but nothin' wet. It'll mildew.
10. Don't waste toilet paper. It costs money. Money don't grow on trees.
11. Flush toilet every time you use it. No excuses, like "I forget," acceptable.
12. (Applies to Jake, mainly:)
    Raise lid before using latrine.
    Lower lid after using.
    (And hit the spot when you aim.)
    P.S. Anyone who don't foller S.O.P. will suffer consequences. (I don't know just what they'll be yet, but don't

worry. I'll think of something—and that's a promise. And you know I don't break promises, and don't forget it either—understand?)

Dan T. Morris
Officer in Command

FIVE
In the Line of Duty

THE days passed quickly as Dan's homemade army fell in line with the military life he taught us. Being on duty got to be routine. Teamwork guided by Dan and his wristwatch caused housecleaning, washing and ironing, making bunks, writing letters to Mama, doing homework, chowtime, and kitchen patrol—all to be completed in orderly fashion.

Clothes were washed in Mama's old wringer washing machine. It took one person on the washer side to poke the clothes through the wringer with a stick, while another person stood at the rinse tub to catch them as they came through the wringer on the other side. Lillian caught whatever Jake sent through the wringer; once, it was a portion of Jake's shirtsleeve—the one he was wearing—and then the tip of Jake's little finger. When

Jake started shouting for help, Dan came and unplugged the wringer, pried it apart, and released the hurt little finger.

Chow was served on time. Meals came straight from Dan's detailed "menu plan." Potatoes were either sliced, diced, chunked, or slivered before they became either pan fried, deep fried, stewed, oven baked, or steamed with pot roast. But the fate of any potato bud always equaled a "tasty 'tater" in the end.

Our most basic breakfast chow, and the favorite of all, was a batch of scrambled eggs along with grits, redeye gravy, country ham, and fat butter biscuits dripping with sourwood honey. In the evening, pinto beans with fatback, spring onions, potatoes, cornbread, and milk made the most favored meal.

Dishwashing teams were appointed to clean the kitchen after chow time. Hank and I made one KP (Kitchen Patrol) team; Elizabeth and Jake, the other team. Hank despised doing dishes. That menial task bored him into the sport of hitting me in a particular place with the wet dishrag while my back was turned and I was bending over to stack pots under the cabinet.

The first yelp from me brought Dan rushing into the kitchen, and Hank was immediately threatened with extra KP. "There are just certain places where you don't pop girls with wet dishrags." From then on, Hank took up the righteous act of singing hymns as he washed dishes to avoid any temptation that could earn him an extra work detail.

Jake was the one who got stuck with extra duty the most. He got it once for making unacceptable noises at the dinner table. Another time, it was for making a similar noise in front of Miz Alexandria, who fell into a "hot flash" from it, and Hank had to help her into a chair. "It's just my age, you know—the change," she fluttered. "I thought I was over it, but it keeps coming back on me. Oh, thank you, Hank. You're such a nice young man."

Jake was quickly exited from the room for both episodes and sentenced to "swab the kitchen deck," which meant to sweep, mop, and wax it. His first wax job took two hours and thirty-two fluid ounces of wax. No one was able to walk into the kitchen for the next six hours. But it *glowed*.

Once Jake was commissioned to do the dishes alone. This time it was for spouting off some off-limit words out in the yard. The preacher had just walked up behind Jake when the words spewed from Jake's mouth. They weren't Sunday school words either. The preacher took it all much better than Dan who stumbled around red-faced and tripped over the two bottom door steps in an attempt to make it into the house.

"Get in the house, boy," Dan ordered Jake. "You can GI the kitchen this evening—alone."

What took the most time was the way Jake stacked them—three miles high with precision and strategy so they would all drip dry.

Jake disliked dishwashing just as much as Hank did. It took the poor boy two-and-a-half hours to wash the dishes, but what took the most time was the way Jake stacked them—three feet high with precision and strategy, so they would all drip dry. His engineering made a beautiful arrangement on the kitchen counter. Tea cups dangled from pot handles, which jutted out in all directions over the plates underneath. Wooden spoons, sticking out here and there, served as grand poles on which to perch glasses upside down. It would have been a shame to see Jake's work of art fall apart. It's a good thing a train didn't pass through until after Elizabeth had put them all away. Jake was taking a much deserved break and was about to admire his masterpiece when I called him to the homework table.

"Jake, you've been in that kitchen long enough," I said. "Lillian, honey, stop chewing on your pencil."

"But I have nerves," she said.

"Nonsense, you're too little to be nervous," I said.

"Arithmetic makes me have nerves and makes me chew my pencil," Lillian said.

"Well, it's not good for your teeth, and it also has germs on it. Germs cause worms, the old people say. Your pencil looks like you leave it every night with a pack of hungry field mice, so don't gnaw on it anymore now."

"Can I chew bubble gum then?" Lillian asked.

"No, Ma'am, you may not chew gum either. You blow bubbles in my face while I'm trying to help you with your homework. You forget to spit it out before going to bed and then it falls out on your pillow, and I end up having to cut a chunk of your hair out. Bubble gum does not look nice stuck in your hair, Lillian— neither do gaps."

Jake came to the table, blowing his nose. "I 'bleeve I've blown most all my brains into a hanky. Wish I didn't have allergies."

"Where are your books?" I asked.

"At school. We didn't have homework tonight."

"That's nice. We'll see by your report card if that's so. Then you can go take your bath," I said.

Next to church pews and extra KP, the bathtub was Jake's worst enemy, but I was in charge of seeing that everyone kept Dan's commandment that "cleanliness is next to godliness," so I pointed Jake to the direction of the "latrine."

"Shucks, do I hafta?" Jake groaned.

"Yes, you have to! Now march," I demanded.

"But I like my dirt, Mel."

"It's a sin to go dirty, Jake. Says so in the Bible," I preached. "Lillian, stop chewing your nails, honey."

"Where in the Bible does it say that?" Jake asked. "I ain't never read it."

"Never mind where, and don't say *ain't*. It'll make your teacher faint. Now, go take

your bath and don't forget to put on clean
underwear—some that don't have holes in
them."

"Most all my underdrawers have holes
in 'em," Jake said.

"Then get Elizabeth to mend them for
you. Dan does not want us to wear
underwear with holes—in case we get in
an accident and have to go to the
hospital," I said.

"I know, I know. He don't want us to
get caught with holy underwear, 'cause
nothin's s'posed to be holier than the
Bible," Jake said.

"That's right, Jake, especially your
underwear," I confirmed.

"Why, that'd be another sin for you,
Jake," Lillian added.

"I wish I could catch *you* sinnin' just
once, Melanie!" Jake said. "Then you'd
want to sin some more."

At those words, I jumped up, grabbed
Jake by the ear, and ushered him into the
bathroom.

Lillian wound up her homework with a
letter to Mama. Elizabeth helped with
some of the spelling, but only when Lillian
asked. Lillian usually spelled words just as
I did—the way they sounded. It took her
an eternity to write a single letter. Lillian
always had much to say.

Even though Lillian had been totally
blind in one eye since birth, no one could
tell it by looking at her. She worked extra
hard to make up for it, by excelling in
everything, even arithmetic, which she
achieved by listening and simply

The homework brigade

absorbing everything around her. How many other six-year-olds could remember nearly every word the preacher said on Sunday mornings, even if they didn't know exactly what it all meant? That's why she knew almost every hymn in the Broadman Hymnal by heart already! Lillian could read—out of the eye that was not blind—as well as any other six-year-old. She hardly mentioned her blindness and once indicated that she would never have known the difference if she hadn't been told.

I read Lillian's "newsletter to Mama" aloud for us all to enjoy:

Dear Mama,

My dog Frisky can no longer stay in the house. He makes Jake sneeze. He jumps on Miz Alexandria and licks her in the face. His fleas got on Miz Alexandrias fur peace and she had to get it dee-flead. Then the preecher came by and Frisky nearly bit him. Dan waz fit to be tied, but Frisky waz tied to his leash that I waz holding. That saved the preecher!

One morning Frisky made Hank late for a job tri-out. Pore Frisky had an acident in Hanks shoe and Hank put his foot in it! Dan got mad and Hank got nervus, cause no one is ever spoze to be late for anything, specialy work.

Jake got a new horn. Melanie said it sounded like a dying cow and that it waznt new but old as the hills, that somebody fooled Jake. He played the new horn for Miz Alexandria. Jake sez people riskt their lives when they come to our house but he waz joking! Hank sez we are an advenchure. I think so two. I wish you were hear with us. We miss you alot Mama.

Dan is bilding Frisky a doghouse outside. Hes making a reel dog manchun for Frisky and sed he wood paint it red.

Pleeze come home soon.

*Love
Lillian*

PS. I love you xxxxooooxxxxoooo

SIX
A Private First-class Bloomer

WE were thankful for two things in
Dan's homemade army. One was not
having to rise to the sounds of reveille
coming from a bugle. Then one day Jake
brought home a funny-looking horn he'd
found for twenty-five cents in the base-
ment of the thrift store. It made a loud
sound that was horrible and powerful
enough to set off an earthquake. That's
why Dan stuck to his own mouthpiece for
reveille.

We called the sounds which came from
Jake's horn, his "unacceptable noises."
No one could stand them, and it was
apparent that everyone was going to grow
up deaf if they didn't cease. Jake said that
no one appreciated his music—which was
true—and that no one around our house
had any "call of the wild" spirit—which

*. . . Jake sez people riskt their lives when
they come to our house, . . . but Hank sez
we are an advenchure!*

was also true. The horn was one sure way to drive off any unwanted invaders from our fort. After Jake's trial runs with the bargain horn, hearing "Rise and shine. Hit the deck. Haul out on the double and move it, move it, move it" was music to our ears!

The second thing we were thankful for not having to do in Dan's homespun army was marching around the house, clicking our heels together the way he sometimes did, practicing his drills and saying "Hut, two, three, four—hut, two, three, four." Whenever Dan did that, we just looked at him, wondering what made him tick and how he could be so wrapped up in it all. His eyes always focused straight ahead with a faraway look, like he was some-place else—guarding the tomb of the unknown soldier or marching before the President. He wasn't aware that anyone else was around when he marched back and forth through the house that way. He hardly moved an eyelid. For someone who wasn't fond of formal situations, he was sure formal when it came to his patri-otism. I think the American flag is the only thing that could make Dan cry.

Respect, humility, and love toward God, country, and fellowman are just a few of the things we learned from Dan, and that was a lot. We learned them mostly from observation, because Dan never said much, but it was all in the air. You could feel it so strong that you could almost smell it, like smelling history in old historic places.

There were only two things that Dan

could never teach me. One was how to do push-ups and the other was how to tell time. Once when I was younger, Dan had spent an entire evening trying to teach me the time of day. He repeatedly changed the hands of an old broken alarm clock with the front glass off. I was supposed to tell him what time it was whenever he moved the hands around, but I just didn't understand the face of a clock at all. Dan felt that a person should learn to do something the very first time he was shown it. Dan wasn't patient along those lines, and we both became terribly frustrated. Finally Dan just put the clock away and gave that stern look which belonged to him and him only.

Much later on, I was standing in front of a clock, and all the things that Dan had tried to teach me three years before suddenly became crystal clear. Understanding the face of a clock now seemed as simple as turning on a light. Hank said that my timing in the understanding of simple matters was due to the fact that I stepped to a "different drummer," whatever that meant. He said for me not to feel so bad that it had taken me three years to learn how to tell time.

"Melanie," he told me. "You'll be happy to know that Emily Dickinson never knew what time it was until she was fifteen, and she never asked anybody because she was ashamed to. But look what she went on to do in life with all those poems she wrote. The one I like best is how she would not have lived in vain if she could help just one fainting robin into his nest again.

Then there's the one about truth:

*Tell the truth, but tell it slant. . . . with
explanation kind.*
*The truth must dazzle gradually or every
man go blind.*

I believe Hank practiced that one on truth. He could be spectacular at times, imitating anybody he wanted to, and what a showman he was.

Dan never made us salute or say, "Yes, sir," though we often said it out of respect and sort of unconsciously, too, mainly because Dan seemed so much more grown up and seemed to deserve that kind of respect. It was something we did on our own, sometimes without even thinking about it. Dan did like for our shoes to have spit-shines, especially on the Lord's Day, and he instructed how this was done the army way.

The only time Dan had us marching was when we went to church, and this was serious business in Dan's book, so the marching just came naturally as we followed the path to church. Jake and I often fell out of step, but that was because we marched at the rear. Dan must have had eyes in the back of his head, or else he could tell by our footsteps, because he always knew when someone was out of step. Most of the time he said so, adding that none of us would ever make it past a PFC (Private First Class) if we didn't learn to stay in step.

Jake once tried to tell Dan that people

ought to go to church any other day of the week except Sunday, because Sunday was the Lord's day off. He said it was in the Bible how the Lord took one day a week off, and if people read their Bibles like they ought to, they'd know the Lord was on vacation when Sunday rolled around. Jake's solution to this age-old tradition was that we have services at home on a weekday with Hank as the preacher.

"Hank's already baptized us all anyway," Jake said, "in the big ditch next to Daddy's honey house, when he was pretending to be Grandpa one day, after a gully-washer rain came and turned the ditch into a reglar river. It was right after one of those summer flash floods came," Jake reminisced.

Jake had our homemade church services all figured out. "Lil can lead the singing. Liz and Melanie can sing duets. Then we could all be the congregation while Hank preaches." Jake even offered to say "Amen" a couple times now and then, because he knew Dan wouldn't say it. Jake also promised not to sneeze, clear his throat, scratch his ears, chew his nails, or wiggle around while Hank was preaching.

Nobody went for Jake's suggestion about changing Sunday around. We knew Jake would choose going to church any day of the week over sitting in a schoolroom all daylong. Jake really beat all sometimes. Like the old saying goes, "He was like an old rabbit in the briar patch while we were the possums up a gum tree."

We spent half the day on Saturday

getting ready for Sunday, washing our hair, spit-shining our shoes, studying our Bible lessons, learning verses, and taking baths. Jake also took a bath on Saturday—"whether he needed it or not!" His memorization of verses created entire new versions of the Bible! He hoped that somebody would someday write a version with words that even he could understand!

I guess we bloomed the brightest on Sunday with our spit-shined shoes, the boys in their suits and we girls in our blue linen spring coats, the "dusters," which Mama had made each Easter. But not this year. Elizabeth's duster was the only one that still seemed to fit the way it should. Everything always seemed to fall in place for her!

It was still cool enough on Sunday spring mornings and evenings for those coats, even though mine and Lillian's were now out of proportion to our bodies. We'd be glad when Mama could come home and make us new ones or adjust our present dusters to our current shapes.

SEVEN
Sunday Maneuvers

GOING to church was not second nature to Dan at this point in time, since he'd become more accustomed to pup-tents than church pews on Sunday. But since Mama wanted us in church on Sundays, Dan made sure we were there, and on time, too! I was certain that Dan had now come to feel more comfortable on old forgotten battlefields than in churches, but he tried to set the example for us. It wasn't easy for a twenty-one-year-old to get five overly active young folks onto a church pew on time.

With a look of agonizing pain, Dan marched our little brigade up the trodden and not-straight-but-narrow path which led to church. We went across the big ditch that became a baptismal gully during flash floods and then behind the honey house where Daddy once extracted

Sunday maneuvers

sourwood and clover syrup from the honeycombs. Our path wound through the Piedmont Apiaries as Daddy's bee yards had been called; behind Mr. Pittman's place; up by Uncle Will's barnyard, horse stables, and store; past the Watts' place; the Dolittles'; the Nelms'; and finally across the street to the church. We'd worn a grassless line, but no one seemed to complain!

Dan maneuvered us into the first totally empty pew closest to the back door. This wasn't so Dan could make a quick exit after the last "Amen" was said, but to keep his little army band from disturbing anyone. Dan sat erect in church with his arms folded. He yielded to the pew once he was in it and shaped himself to fit its wooden form. He seemed to feel even more secure once his eyes were focused straight ahead toward the preacher. His forward gaze changed only occasionally to give threatening glares at Jake or Lillian, but mostly at Jake.

Jake was eternally blessed with two sermons on Sunday: one from the preacher and one from Dan. It was next to impossible for Jake to sit glued to a church pew for long. The first note of organ music was the signal for Jake's right leg to start swinging back and forth or gyrating up and down. Church pews tortured Jake so that his nerves popped out in all sorts of forms: from hiccups and yawning, sneezing and sniffles, to throat-clearing and nail-chewing. Raised eyebrows or frowns from Dan only slowed down or modified the action of whatever was plaguing Jake at the moment.

Strange itches were the most dreaded symptoms that Jake developed in church. They usually began with his nose and spread to other out-of-the-way places on his body. He could not resist the urge to scratch wherever it itched, so he did. Getting to the itch sometimes involved the removal of some parts of his clothing, such as his coat and bow tie and even his shoes. Jake's dilemma affected all of us in various ways. Lillian giggled, Elizabeth pretended she didn't see or hear, Hank turned red, Dan was worse than mad, and I was glad we were sitting at the back.

Lillian had few problems in church, except for giggling at Jake. She showed off by whispering and pointing in perfect harmony, especially during the choir anthem. Between Jake on one side of me and Lillian on the other, I was driven up the wall, across the ceiling, and back down the other side.

Lillian observed everything in church while she still managed to absorb most of the preacher's good words. She'd call my attention to everything she noticed: "Did you see that fly buzz right under Mr. Watts's nose and wake him up just then? Look at those fake flowers in Mrs. Reed's hat. Real flowers would look much better, wouldn't they? Don't you wish we could sit at the front next to the stained-glass window with Daddy's name on it?"

I managed to answer all her questions by shaking my head to mean yes or no or by shrugging my shoulders to mean I didn't know at all.

Standing up for congregational hymns was usually a pleasant change from the confusion created by Lillian and Jake. That is, unless I was sharing a songbook with Hank, who especially loved to sing hymns and knew at least three of all the harmony parts. He usually started out singing baritone. Then he'd switch back and forth from bass to tenor.

I couldn't stay in tune when I sang next to Hank, so I just moved my mouth and pretended to be singing. This always caused Lillian to say, "You aren't singing. Why are you moving your mouth like you're singing when you aren't making a sound?" Dan rarely looked at a songbook in church—only straight ahead. Elizabeth managed a hymnal all to herself. Lillian already knew most of the words, and Jake hummed along or tapped his foot to the melodies.

It was amazing that Jake and Lillian were so well behaved when anyone prayed aloud in church. Lillian was fascinated with prayers. Jake respected them. The last "Amen" came soon after the choir sang "Just As I Am," and it meant that soon we'd all be heading home to peel potatoes.

When the organ sounded its dismissal chords, Dan made tracks for home. We were all supposed to follow suit, but we weren't as quick as Dan when it came to getting out of church. Hank lingered to chat and to shake hands with everyone who had been in church that day.

It was my job to keep Lillian and Jake from escaping and getting lost in the crowd once we were out in the churchyard. While Hank was being congenial, my arms would be jerked from their sockets in a struggle to keep Lillian and Jake from running off somewhere.

Elizabeth would stand close to Hank and pretend she didn't even know me and my two Sunday show-offs. Sometimes I wondered how on earth Elizabeth had ended up in "our" family. In fact I sometimes wondered how the whole lot of us had ended up in the same family. We were all so different. I think there were others around who may have thought that, too, but no one ever came right out and said it.

One thing everybody could see was the deep spiritual thread that bound us all together—a thread that could never be broken, not in this world nor the one to come. That's how complete strangers could recognize us as "one."

Sometimes people who had known only Daddy would stop us on the street and say, "I know you are W. F. Morris's children. There is just something about you that says so." Some people once came up to us girls and said, "You have to be related to Desma Morris [Daddy's only sister]. You all look just like her." Not one of us girls favored each other much, but when people said that, it pleased Aunt

Desma. Mama had sometimes wondered if people ever gave her an ounce of credit for having us!

Anyway, while everyone was milling around outside church, I'd manage a few "Good mornings" between twists and turns with Lillian and Jake.

On the way home from church once I suggested to Hank that he become a politician. "You really do have a special way of making everyone feel important, Hank. You'd make a perfect politician. Why, everybody in the church would vote for you!"

Hank smiled and said, "I know it."

"We didn't rush you off or anything, did we, Hank?" I asked. "I mean, you didn't miss speaking to anyone, did you?"

"No, don't think I missed a soul, except for a few choir members who got out the side door."

"Gosh, I don't want you to get the reputation of slighting people, Hank. Do you think we should go back and catch those choir members?"

"No, they just lost out today," he said yawning. "Everybody else got to see me." Hank spoke with complete self-assurance and didn't sound irritating as most other people might.

"Did anybody ask you about Mama?" I asked.

"Yes, they did," Hank answered confidentially. "And I told them the same thing I told Miz Alexandria, 'Mama should be home in a week or two.'"

"Oh, Lord, Hank. I don't know if you're

saying the right thing or not."

"Of course I am. Just wait and see. If you keep thinking on something and saying it's going to happen, it'll happen."

"Oh, I don't know, Hank."

"Sure, thinking hard on something is about like praying hard for something," Hank said. "It's the attitude you do it in. That's why a person ought to be careful what he prays for, 'cause he just might get it, whether he wants it or not."

Lillian became animated at the word *prays*. "Mama says you have to put feet on your prayers if you want 'em to work for you."

"Lillian, honey," Hank said. "I not only put feet on my prayers, I put roller skates on 'em." A prayer on roller skates? Well, it could be if Hank said so!

We all arrived home just in time to peel the potatoes, onions, and carrots for Dan's Sunday stew. I got to peel the onions.

Jake took his tongue-lashing from Dan like a real trooper. His wrinkled Sunday jacket changed into a small coat of armor. He stood bravely, with crooked bowtie, shirttail out, hands in his sagging pockets, and eyes glued to the floor, as he shifted from one foot to the other. Dan looked so funny pacing up and down dressed in Mama's Sunday apron, delivering his sermon to Jake.

"Why if Daddy was alive, he'd flail the dickens right out of you, Jake, 'specially if you'd been layin' up for one of his hard lickens."

Dan didn't let up an inch until Jake

had heard his sermon through. "Grandpa Harris would roll over in his grave, if he saw how you act in church."

Grandpa Harris had been a Baptist minister with the proud record of being the founder of over twenty-five Baptist churches.

Dan described Grandpa Harris as "a great preacher man who was long-winded, kept you in church meetings 'til two in the afternoon, and wound up his sermons with dinner on the grounds or with baptismal services down by the river. By then it was time to go back to church for BYPU [Baptist Young Peoples Union] and an evening of singing hymns.

"You didn't fool around while Grandpa Harris was preachin', or he'd stop right in the middle of his sermon and upbraid you in front of the whole congregation. Why, I'd ruther had a whoppin' any day than one of Grandpa's thunder-boltin' sermons and tongue-floggins. You'd better be glad, Jake, that it's not one a Grandpa's sermons you're havin' to sit through on a Sunday, or you wouldn't draw a breath for three hours or more, much less think about scratchin' your ear. And another thing, just because Grandpa slept in a toboggan [cap] at night to keep his bald head warm, it don't mean he couldn't get hot when it came to religion or politics."

I just knew Jake was going to catch more than a tongue-whipping someday. It had been breathed into Dan that "to spare the rod was to spoil the child." Daddy had spared the rod from none of us, and oh, how it hurt. Why you could just feel the dickens himself coming right out of you. Mama had said that when Daddy's temper got riled, all purgatory broke loose. He was a fiery person when his embers got stirred, and when they flamed up, they were a long time in dying down. That was when Daddy would use the rod on us. Daddy's rod had come from Mama's huge weeping willow tree—appropriately named for the purpose. Those willowy branches stung terribly. Daddy's "keen little hickory stick" could have also been called a "humble stick." Whenever one broke, *we* had to go out and fetch a new one! I could never understand it when Daddy would say before every switching, "Now, this is going to hurt *me* more than it hurts you, but you won't know what that means until you're as old as I am." At the time, I did not believe a single word of that.

Something told me that Dan could have the same powers with the rod that Daddy once had, but Dan never used them.

EIGHT
Sabbath Day Invasions

DAN declared the Sabbath a day of rest, but nobody rested at our house, unless he'd fallen asleep or sick. The seventh day of the week was as busy as any other day. Only the atmosphere was different— Sunday afternoons brought a host of visitors to our home.

Dan's longtime friend, J. L. Davis, showed up once after Sunday dinner and brought Lillian a puppy, which was Dan's gift to her from "overseas." It had come from over the hill instead of overseas, but Lillian didn't question where it really came from. She named her new pet "Frisky" and loved it immediately.

Whenever JL came to the house, or was even thought about, the story of Moses in the bulrushes often came to mind. He and JL had one thing in common—they'd both been found in little baskets. JL was found on the steps of a church on the very morning that the church had made a covenant to start the local children's home. When the covenant had been sealed, a childless, middle-aged couple in the congregation knew that the little baby in the basket had been sent to bring them joy in their remaining days. They adopted JL and their lives were indeed made richer. The love expressed by that one church has since been multiplied through the years for countless thousands who have benefited from the orphanage home.

The good Lord had watched out for JL Could any of us children doubt that He would watch out for us too? It was something I thought about—long and hard.

Grandpa and Grandma Morris, in their middle seventies, would drive from the neighboring county in their flashy '36 Chevrolet. Grandpa always dressed "fit to kill" on Sunday, except for an ancient old hat that he could never throw away.

Grandpa and Grandma always got the red carpet welcome. In fact, whenever kindred hearts or favored kinsmen came calling at our house, they were met by a very loud welcoming committee of five or six youngsters, depending on how many of us were home when the visitors arrived. We'd crash through the back door, skip all six back steps, and land feet first. After surrounding the visitors, we'd hug them "from the knees up," beginning with Lillian, the youngest, who could reach hardly higher than the knees. Then towering above her was Jake, who gave big bear hugs wherever he could find a place. Elizabeth would gently embrace all

dearly beloved ones right at the waist.
Soaring above her were Hank and me. We
hugged everybody around the neck,
shoulders, and arms. Dan, like the perfect
Southern gentleman he was, always had
more restraint and waited his turn in the
background.

"We'd a gotten here sooner," Grandpa
said one time, "but your Grandma won't
let me drive over twenty miles an hour."

"Well, Mart, if you'd fix that awful hole
in the floor on my side of the car, I could
stand to go faster," Grandma said. "Seeing
the road flying under my feet makes me
swimmy-headed and dizzy."

Grandpa brought Lillian and Jake a
king-size soda and a candy bar to share
between them. The soda was the best treat.
Daddy had never allowed carbonated water
in the house. Lillian and Jake turned the
doom of sharing into a sport. They made a
game of taking Daddy's yardstick to
measure the candy bar before dividing it
equally. A measuring cup served to
distribute the fair-and-square portions of
carbonated water.

"Well, I never saw youngins go to such
extremes to get their fair helpin's of a sody
pop!" Grandpa exlaimed.

"Oh, Mart, hush now. They're just
playin'. Besides, it keeps down any
arguin'," Grandma said defensively. She
patted Lillian and Jake on the head and
reminded them, "Never act ugly over such
small things as chewing gum, sodas, and

Grandpa and Grandma—favorite invaders

candy bars, for 'pretty is, as pretty does.'"
That was Grandma's motto. A real fine
lady, she was, and Elizabeth was heir to
the same distinction.

Grandpa never sat anywhere long.
"How's your Mama doin' up in the
hospital?" he always asked, looking
distressed as he walked around. Ever since
Daddy, their middle son, had died, it
seemed that his and Grandma's health
had gone downhill too. They would've
given anything to get out to see her, but
the trip would've been too hard on them,
frail as they were.

Grandpa said he and Grandma had too
many miles on them already to go far
from home—they did well to see about us
on Sundays. He said their "spizzerinktum"
[pep] had all been spent—in other words,
their "get-up-and-go had got up and
went." They feared traveling very far, and
Mama was a long way from home.

"Mama's doin' fine, Grandpa," Dan
would answer.

"I'm sure glad you're home, Dan. Me
and your Grandma don't have to fret
ourselves so much anymore. Now we'll be
able to sleep 'of a night,' but we'll sleep
tolerable better when your Mama gets
home. When do you allow she's comin'
home?"

Hank answered the question right away,
but with more reservation one time. It was
harder to fib to Grandpa than it was to
outsiders. "Ummm, as soon as Dan gets a
new car, we're going to get Mama." No
one corrected Hank—not even Dan.

Grandma wrapped her shawl tightly about her and picked up her walking cane. "I hope that won't be too long," she said. "Me and your Grandpa are gettin' too old to worry over you all like we've been worryin'. Now you all mind your brother."

"We will," Jake and Lillian said in unison.

"Grandma," Lillian said, "we write letters to Mama. She hasn't had time to answer them yet."

"Keep writin' and she'll answer when she's able," Grandma said hugging her.

Grandpa reached for his worn old hat. "I 'spect we better be goin'."

Grandma remarked as she often did, "Lawsy mercy, Mart, I do wish you'd buy yourself a new hat!"

"Awh, shaw, Mitt, what's wrong with this one? It's 'fair to midlin' so far as I'm concerned. I'll buy one. Just give me time," Grandpa said, lighting a cigarette.

Grandma shook her head and laughed with her eyes. "And those cigarettes, Mart. I'm afraid they're goin' to be the death of you."

"Awh, Mitt, you know I only smoke once a week. That won't hurt. Besides they're better 'n snuff and ain't half as dusty," Grandpa reasoned.

Any signs of snuff, including spittoons, at Grandma's house were fairly well hidden but my cousin and I just happened across a snuff can one day. It was just sitting there on the shelf, tempting us to try it. Grandma found us both deathly ill and put us to bed with cold cloths on our heads. Our dreaded illnesses were diagnosed by the traces of brown powder on our mouths. We confessed the whole wicked deed to a loving grandmother, who understood every trait of human nature, including curiosity for snuff.

Hank had an array of friends that made our backyard resemble a used car lot on Sunday. They came in from the other side of town and from all sides of the tracks and in all shapes and sizes. It didn't matter to Hank, so long as they merited his friendship, and anyone who liked Hank always fit the bill. Jake said, "Hank treats all human beans the same." And Hank did.

One of Hank's friends was extra special. I looked for him all afternoon and was about to give up, when finally he appeared like Prince Charming out of a storybook. It wasn't exactly the preacher who inspired me so much on Sunday, but Hank's friend, David Samuel Deyton. Even his name was poetic. I could hardly draw a breath from the moment he arrived and felt I was about to faint during his entire visit, though I never did. Now and then I went to my room to catch a good deep breath.

"What's ailin' you?" Jake asked when I nearly knocked him down in the hallway, trying to make it to my room. "You've had this funny color on your face for about an hour now."

"Color? Oh, what color?" I asked, clasping my face with both hands.

"Red—a weird red—that's what color,"

Jake noted bluntly. "What's the matter, Melanie? Does ole D. Sammy Deyton do that to you?"

"No—no, he doesn't," I fibbed.

"You can't kid me, Melanie. You didn't turn that awful sick color 'til he got here—and the way you look at him. . . ."

I was getting angry at Jake now for prying into my heart. "Jake, your remarks are sometimes too lickety-split for your own good," I said. "Too hasty, you know. They are also tactless and uncultured."

"Well, excuse me, 'Miz Respectability,'" Jake said, bowing. "All I can say for you, Mel, is that I'm sure glad you have some scattered brains. If it wern't for that, you'd be plum dull to be around most all the time."

I felt my face getting hot and redder. "You know, Jake, you are downright murderous to the English language, and it ought to be unlawful the way you speak out your thoughts so, especially when you don't know what you're talking about!"

I was in my room by this time and about to slam the door. Jake was looking at me with a devilish grin on his face. "Just one more thing, Jake. I don't want to hear any more of your opinions on me, especially on Sunday. Why, it's just disrespectful. That's what it is. And since we're on the subject of respect, I want more of it from you—from now on."

Respect was a big word we'd all heard from the day we were born. Daddy had said, "All we have is respect and our name." He spent a lot of time drumming that into us, too. It was pecked out on our brains. None of us would ever let go of it without a fight.

I wanted to forget my run-in with Jake. If I put all my thoughts on my brother's best friend, it was easy to forget all else. Seeing him on Sunday carried me through the whole week. Just glancing at him left me with heart palpitations, a terrible cold sweat, tongue-tiedness, a funny sick color, and loss of appetite for the next three days.

NINE
The Blitz on Romance

SINCE Hank's hopes always ran high, his positive attitude never failed to rub off on all those around him. Only once did I see another side of Hank that I'd never seen before. But it influenced me so that I buried all my hopes in the backyard and almost threw myself in after them.

It all came about just because Hank needed a pencil. "Hey, Melanie, do you have a pencil I can borrow? Lillian has chewed on half of mine and broken the lead on the rest of them."

"Sure, Hank, come on in. Now, I know I have some extra pencils here somewhere," I said, digging around in my dresser drawer for them.

My back was turned for only a moment when curious Hank uncovered my hopes and dreams. "What's this?" he asked, unfolding a paper labeled "Poetry." "I didn't know you were a poet, Mel."

Horror struck me, and I whirled to reach

The blitz
on romance

for my cherished paper. Too late! Hank was a speed reader. I felt myself turning that awful, sick color again. I reached for the paper again, but Hank raised it further and further from my hand, as he read my precious writing. I knew I was going to be the first fourteen-year-old to die of a heart attack or a stroke. I prayed for both to strike me. My stomach was getting sicker by the minute.

Hank's reaction to my literary composition told me that I had committed one of the worst crimes I could against my dear brother. "I'm shocked at you, Melanie! It's just unheard of. My best friend—of all people! I just won't stand for it. The guys I know do not allow their kid sisters to carry torches for their best friends. You can put any romantic notions for my friends out of your head. First of all, they're too old for you, and second of all, I know my friends better than you do."

Hank's friends were no more than three years older than I, but in this case, three years amounted to three decades to Hank. He firmly enforced the law—I was never to have any romantic notions about any of his friends again. The saddest part was that Hank was everybody's friend. He even had friends on desert islands and at the North Pole. Hank stated clearly that it would not be good for my health to develop any more dreamy eyes which ventured to "admire someone from afar, unless they were as far away as Jupiter or Mars."

"You won't tell anyone, will you, Hank?"

I begged in a cracking voice. "Especially your best friend?"

"Tell anyone? Do you think I want my friends to know that I have a kid sister who'd write something like this!" Hank said, shaking my poem in the air. "I can't believe it, Mel! Just listen to this: *Oh, David, you are truly a marvel . . . carved from the purest of marble.* Let me tell you, Melanie. No friend of mine is pure. Someday you'll understand and someday you'll thank me."

Never, I thought. *I'll die first, probably at the age of ninety, a crabby old maid, with a broken hip, childless and abandoned by my family, with no one to care for me but other regretful old maids in a home for lonely hearts. But no one would miss me seventy-six years from now.* I made Hank no reply.

Hank's words were the last straw—the one that broke the proverbial camel's back. There was nothing left to do but end it all. My anticipated heart attack and stroke never came, even though I prayed hard for both of them. Hank had crushed me with his words, which were worse than any death. My wonderful brother had never spoken to me or to anyone that I knew of, so cruelly. My knees weakened, and I fell into choking sobs with nothing to comfort me but the bedpost.

I could never face Hank or anyone else again. I drew myself up and walked to the window. *Hank will be sorry for being so mean to me*, I thought, *when I am dead and gone.* I could see him weeping and crying as he viewed my poor dead body all stretched out in a coffin. I could just see the whole tragic scene in my mind. . . .

. . . There they were—together at my funeral—Hank and his best friend, weeping over me. Hank was sobbing, "My poor little sister is dead, and it's all my fault . . . Boo hoo hoo, sob, sob—choke."

David Deyton was consoling my grieving brother. "Don't blame yourself, Hank. Oh, isn't she lovely lying there—the best she's ever looked, Hank, resting so peacefully? Oh, it's all so tragic."

"Oh, Lord—Lord, forgive me!" Hank was wailing and blew his nose into a soggy, yellowed hanky.

David Deyton wept, then fell over my casket, kissed my hands, and lifted me up in his arms, soaking my lovely white dress with his tears. "How I loved her!" he groaned. Hank fell to the floor, unconscious, and both of them were carried away.

I came back to reality, mourning for myself over the tragedy of it all. My funeral was the saddest one I'd ever witnessed.

Soon it would all come true:

She fell from her window to an untimely death, and was found with a broken neck, back, and wrist.

I looked at the ground below me—nearly a five-foot drop. Lillian could leap from that window and clamor back up without a bruise. It wouldn't work to jump into anything.

103

An overdose, I thought. The most poisonous thing Mama kept in the house was castor oil. Just the taste of it would kill me if suffocation from holding my nose didn't do it first. There had to be a more painless way to die. But it had to be tragic—very tragic—and sad.

Aspirin would be painless enough—a whole bottle downed by a glass of water—with no bad aftertaste. I tiptoed to the medicine cabinet and reached behind Raleigh's Linament and Dr. Miles' Nervene for the aspirin. Three white pills were left in the bottle. Just enough to kill an aching head, but not enough to take away my aching heart. I felt cheated.

Suddenly the house rumbled. A whistle blew in the distance. Old Number Nine was southbound, roaring down the tracks. I could throw myself in front of a train, and it would all be over—except for picking up all the little pieces of me scattered from here to Cook's Crossing. Oh, but then, David Deyton couldn't say, "Isn't she lovely lying there?" and I couldn't take that away from him or from myself. It would be tragic all right—too tragic for my own liking. My mind was cluttered with too much detail. I'd go to bed and think about it tomorrow. To just up and die was not all that easy. No wonder such matters were left up to heaven.

Time heals all wounds, or so they say, but during certain times of the year nothing healed, according to Grandma. Old folks called them "dawg days," when a scratch on your arm stayed with you for months and never seemed to heal until the signs were right for healing. I never seemed to come under that sign, so I took up the cross of a life from which love and romance had been blitzed forever.

Whenever the handsome hero of my youth paid my brother a visit, I resorted to hiding in my room or the bathroom. Never again did my eyes meet the eyes of the one who had first inspired me to be a poet. But I tucked away the initials *D.S.D.* into a small corner of my heart for safe keeping.

TEN
Our Tin Lizzy Car:
The Army Tank

"COME quick! You've got to see it!"
Lillian yelled, charging into my room.

"What is it, Lil?" I asked.

"You'll just have to see it!" she said,
panting for breath. "It's the biggest one
I've ever seen, and it's green—army green.
It's out in our backyard!"

"Oh, Lord—a snake. You've seen a big
green snake in the yard!" I gasped.

"No, not a snake. It's bigger than a
snake, and we can all get in it at the
same time," she said, leading me to the
back door.

"Oh, a tent—an army tent," I said.

"No, just look. Isn't it huge?" Lillian
said, pointing ahead.

That was slightly underestimating the
shape of what Lillian had pointed to in
the backyard. Not only was it big and
green, but it was also old and ugly—the
ugliest car in the world was sitting in our

"Come quick! You've got to see it!"

backyard! I got motion sickness from just looking at it.

"It's our new car!" she cried out.

"Ummm, did you say 'new,' Lillian?" I asked.

"Well, it's all new to us," she replied innocently.

Hank was walking around the "new" car, giving it love pats and spit-shines here and there. "Come on out and take a look at her!" Hank yelled. "Isn't she a real baby?"

Yes—a baby tank, I thought.

"Hey, what's that big rusty thing sticking out all across the front of her?" Jake shouted, as he approached from the neighbor's yard.

"It's a sun visor," Hank answered. "Few cars have them anymore."

"But it's all rusted—gollee, the whole car's rustin' up," Jake said, getting closer. "What're you gonna do 'bout all those rust spots, Hank?"

"Oh, sand 'em down maybe and paint her someday, but for now she's just what we need. Those rust spots blend right in with the green to give her that army-camouflage look," Hank said proudly.

"Who wants to be camouflaged?" Jake asked. "But I guess we'll have to be, if we're really going to ride around in that thing. Where'd it come from, anyways?"

"It's left over from World War I, the Korean War, and World War II," I said. "First, it was a wrecked submarine tank; then it was salvaged from a watery grave and converted to a land tank; then it was labeled an army reject; and then. . . ."

". . . That's not very humorous, Melanie," Hank interrupted, "Dan brought it home today."

"From where?" I asked. "The Army-Navy Surplus Store?"

"No, Melanie, but Dan got a bargain—a real bargain, or . . . ."

". . . He would never have bought it," Elizabeth said, skipping down the back door steps.

"Hey, now, isn't she a beaut?" Hank asked Elizabeth.

"Yes, she is a brute," Elizabeth answered. "Doesn't everyone think so?"

"Yeah," Jake chimed. "I thought it was a bulldozer at first, because of that big sun-visor thing."

"Now, look, you all," Hank said. "I'm going to be the driver of this car most of the time, and none of you will ride in it if you don't behave."

"Hurray!" Jake shouted. "I'm spared."

"Thank heaven we walk to church," Elizabeth said, looking upward.

"Come on, Liz. You've got to admit the old gal has character. I'll name her after you, Lizzy. How's that?"

"Tin Lizzy Lee," I said. "That's a classy name for an old tank."

Hank got inside the car and cranked the motor. "Sings like a baby, doesn't she?" he yelled. "Hey, listen to the horn. Now get ready. Here she blows."

"WHOO, WHOOOO."

We all jumped back three feet and grabbed our ears. "Dear Lord, it sounds like a freight train," Elizabeth squealed. "It sounds horrible, Hank. An ordinary train sounds better."

"Wanna go for a spin?" Hank yelled, as he backed up old Tin Lizzy Lee.

"No, thanks!" the girls yelled.

"I do," Jake hollered, running to hop in.

"The perfect toy for someone who's been taking Driver's Ed since day one and still can't work a gear shift, wouldn't you say?" Elizabeth asked.

"Yeah, I wonder if he's planning to take some poor girl to the junior-senior prom in that thing?"

"Oh, probably so," Elizabeth answered. "You know Hank. He always comes out smelling like a rose. Anything the car lacks, Hank makes up for with his personality."

Hank's attitude toward the new car rubbed off on everyone but me, and I learned one more grand quality about Elizabeth. She had few complaints about "roughing it" in an old tin can. That young lady could have more endurance for "bedlam in the South" than Scarlett O'Hara. She was as feisty as Scarlett, too, though she'd never jerked the velvet drapes off their royal rods to make a fancy dress as Scarlett once did. Besides, we didn't have velvet drapes!

I dreamed that night of shiny new Fords and Chevrolets. Daddy had always driven long black cars with running boards on the side. I shuddered and nearly sank into tears when I thought of my family riding around town in a car which looked like the twin sister to an army tank.

It wasn't long before we rode to school in Tin Lizzy Lee. I thought it was better than the orange school bus, which made twelve stops between our house and the schoolyard, but I sulked in the back seat. Finally I blurted out, "Daddy would never have bought a car like this!"

"You'd better thank your lucky stars for good old Lizzy here," Hank said. "Daddy had to walk a country mile to school before daylight everyday in freezing blizzards, hail, and snowstorms."

"You left out tornadoes, earthquakes, and flash floods," I added.

"Yes," Elizabeth said, "and he walked barefoot, too. They couldn't afford shoes. Then he had to come home and saw logs until sundown."

"They didn't even have doctors back then," Jake continued. "That's how come Daddy sewed his own foot up with black thread once."

"That's right," Hank said, "and the only thing they had to kill infection with was kerosene or turpentine mixed with brown sugar."

"I thought kerosene was what they used in their oil lamps," Elizabeth said. "They didn't have electricity in Daddy's day."

"Daddy told me that he studied by candlelight—not a kerosene light," Jake said.

By this time, Lillian was almost in tears. "Why didn't my daddy have shoes?" she interrupted. "Didn't they make shoes back then? Why did he have to walk through snowstorms barefoot?"

"Lillian, honey, they are all just trying to make me appreciate the car," I said. "Our daddy had shoes. He went barefoot in the summer because he wanted to, but for winter he had thick leather shoes to keep out the cold. Grandma told me so. She ordered them from the Sears and Roebuck catalog."

"What's that?" Elizabeth tuned in. "I never heard anything about an order catalog. Is that the truth, Hank?"

"Yep, it is," Jake interrupted. "I remember Grandma sayin' it. She ordered all their underdrawers, step-ins, or whatever you call 'em, straight from the catalog. That's where Aunt Desma got her first brassiere—right outta the book."

"Well, it didn't step right 'outta the book,' Jake," said Hank. "Daddy had to walk three miles into town to the post office just to pick up that crazy thing the day it came. I can hear Daddy telling that story now: 'Why, the package was half open and "it" was just a hangin' there, so ah rescued the contraption and stuffed it in my overalls. Ah had no idy what that thing wuz. Couldn't get it all in my breeches, so it hung down outta my pockets and drug the ground them three miles Ah had to go back home.'"

"Poor Daddy," Jake sighed. "I know that's what shortened his days. Can you imagine a poor guy havin' to walk barefoot three miles and with that stuffed in his overalls, too? Ain't that sad, Melanie?"

"Yes, yes, it's all very sad. I've heard enough. I thought we were all allies in the same army. Now you've all turned against me. I don't want to be your lonely enemy. I give in. This car is OK—for scrap yard metal, I guess."

Every passenger in the car turned toward me. "OK, OK, I love her. Is that what you want to hear? But, Hank, you'll never get a date in this old tin jalopy unless you go to the poorhouse to find her."

"Why, Melanie, Melanie, honey," Hank drawled. "You know any girl would jump at the chance to ride in a 'genuwine' antique."

"Why, Hank, *dahlin'* Hank," I drawled back. "I know you have enough charm to sink a battleship, but not enough to get a female into this battle-ax car."

ELEVEN
Army Tank Battles and Blockades

Tin Lizzy Lee squeaked and rattled. She
backfired and blew like a freight train.
People heard us before they saw us and
plugged their ears when we rolled down
the hill. We left a camouflaged green
streak and a puff of gray smoke wherever
we went. Everything was fine until the old
car encountered her first blockade.

We'd all piled into the army tank early
one morning. Hank cranked the motor. It
sputtered and choked.

"What's wrong with you, old girl?" Hank
cooed, as he kept trying to wind her up.
Finally the motor revved, and we plunged
out of the driveway with a few jerks and
forward heaves. Hank was still rusty on
the gearshift, and the jerks and lunges
were enough to make anyone seasick. The
front seat passenger should have been
equipped with a crash helmet. I had an
awful fear of someone going right through

We left a camouflaged green streak and a
puff of gray smoke wherever we went.

the windshield until Hank mastered the gearshift.

We cruised down the road at the momentous speed of thirty-five miles an hour. Then Hank yelled, "Good grief! I knew something was wrong. We're almost out of gas. That's why this baby wouldn't start. Oh, well, I'm sure we'll make it to the gas station. OK, who's got money for gas?"

Nobody answered. "All right, then, everybody can donate some money to the cause. You kids, start coughing up half your ice-cream money. Collect it, Melanie, and don't forget to throw in your half."

"I don't have ice-cream money. I don't even have lunch money," I answered. "Remember—I work in the cafeteria so Dan won't have to give me lunch money."

"Oh, that's right," Hank said. "But I wish you'd give up that job. It just galls me when someone says, 'Hank, didn't I see your kid sister cleaning off tables in the cafeteria today?' I can take people criticizing me, but I don't like them criticizing my family."

"Oh, now you sound like me, Hank. But you'll have to correct your friends next time they say anything. I serve food. I don't clean tables, usually. Do you think I like it? It's that hideous hairnet that I hate. It's supposed to protect the food from falling hairs. I only work in the cafeteria to help Dan out."

"Well, keep your job, then. I'd join you, but I'd look funny in a hairnet. Now that I have some wheels, I'm going to try for a job down at Pike's Drugstore. Since all my friends work there, I'd like it."

Suddenly the old tank gave in to gas-tank hunger, and we started coasting on fumes. The car glided down a hill. "Come on, Lizzy," Hank begged. "Get up enough speed to carry us over that big knoll ahead." We rolled part way up the incline and back down again and rocked back and forth until we stopped dead between the two hills.

"What do we do now?" Lillian asked.

"We get out and push," replied Hank, who didn't budge but gave the orders. "OK, OK, everybody out, except you, Lillian. You might get hit by a car."

"What about the rest of us?" Jake grumbled. "Don't you care if we become victims of a hit-and-run?"

"Stop whining," Hank ordered. "Out, out, all of you, except Lillian. When Dan's not around, you know I give the orders. Do you want to get court-martialed?"

Elizabeth stood outside the car with both hands on her hips. "I don't want to push," she said, stomping her foot. "And I won't. It'll get my clean dress dirty. *You push* and I'll steer."

"You don't have a driver's license," Hank said, "and you can't see over the steering wheel."

"I can sit on everybody's school-books, and I don't need a license in an emergency."

"If you sit on everybody's schoolbooks, then you can't reach the brake pedal," Hank explained.

"OK, OK, stop arguing, you two," I said. "It stands to reason, Hank, that you and Jake should push—you're the only men in the crowd. I can steer and reach the brake pedal."

"OK," Hank mumbled. "I want to get out of here before that school bus comes by and sees us stranded. Come on, Jake, and help me."

With a lot of sweating from Hank and silent grumbling from Jake, we rolled over the next little hill, sailed past Cook's Crossing, and coasted into Trucker's Center where gas was available. Jake and Hank had to run and jump into the car once we got over the hill.

Everyone threw in his change, and Hank ordered up fifty cents' worth of gas. The gas attendant complained, "Why that ain't even worth walking to the pumps for, buddy."

"I know!" Hank laughed. "But you see, sir, we all seem to have forgotten our wallets."

The attendant walked to the pumps, chattering to himself, "Five people in one car, and they all forgot their pocketbooks. It ain't even chicken feed to fill up a tank."

Hank stuck his head out the window. "Fifty cents will carry us a long way in this thrifty car. It couldn't happen again in fifty years."

Hank had to eat those words. The next time we coasted in for gas, it was for forty-five cents' worth. A new gas attendant was on duty. He was standing by the pumps with his back turned. Hank blew the horn. "WHOO, WHOOOO." The attendant's hat went one way and his body went the other. When he got himself together and approached the car, all he could say was "Where'd you git that horn, buddy? I ain't never heard one like it."

"Came right off a freight train," Hank laughed.

"It did make me think that a train done left them tracks over yonder and was comin' right through the middle of this place. Scared me so bad I swallered half my tobaccy," the attendant said.

"It was just us comin' through," Hank said. "We're harmless."

The attendant adjusted his hat and looked Lizzy over for a minute. Then he spat out a big wad of tobacco. "This is what they call one a them dyenosoar cars, ain't it? Say, I knew a rich feller over in Tennessee had a car just like this. His un was pink, though, and it didn't have a horn like this un."

"Yeah, I guess the horns have changed some since then," Hank said grinning. "This must be a newer model."

"Nope, same model, just a different color, but I could be wrong 'bout the horn, though. This was back, oh, some fifteen or twenty years ago. That feller junked his when he got through with it, though."

Hank smiled at the attendant for a few seconds. "Fill her up—with forty-five cents' worth of gas, please."

The attendant shook his head back and forth as he walked to Lizzy's gas tank.

"Shew wee, they's more changed 'bout these cars than the horns. Forty-five cents to fill up a tank this size!"

"Could we please drive on to Mr. Shelton's grocery store?" Elizabeth asked.

"Hey, Hank," Jake called from the back seat. "We could sell this car at Mr. Shelton's Grocery. The only extra piece she'd need is an opener."

Hank frowned. "Opener? What kind of opener?"

"The kind that comes on sardine cans," Jake said. Jake resented giving up his money more than anybody. "I'm not donating to any more causes. The next time we run out of gas, I'll just walk."

"What's happened to old generous Jake?" I asked.

"Yeah, how come you're gettin' so stingy, Jake?" Lillian asked.

"I'm savin' up my money," Jake answered.

"For what?" Elizabeth asked.

"For a while," Jake answered.

"That's no answer!" Elizabeth said, stomping her foot on the floorboard.

Jake crossed his arms. "Well, it's nobody's beeswax," he said stubbornly.

Hmmm, I wondered. *What could old Jake have up his sleeve?* Ordinarily, he'd give the shirt off his back if anybody wanted it, and it wasn't like him not to tell everything he knew. But now, he was tight-mouthed and tight-pocketed. I'd find out—in time—just what Jake was up to.

The barricades encountered by Tin Lizzy Lee were not limited to gas shortages

The backward haul home. . .

alone. However, her endurance throughout
any crisis depended upon the strength and
fortitude of the small army she carried. We
became a human fortress within the green
hunk of steel and metal which transported
us all over town.

The army tank battled scores of blockades following the gas episodes. The list (not counting gas shortages) included: flat tires, spinning hubcaps resembling small UFOs, dead batteries, broken water hoses, perpetual backfiring, leaks, an explosion under the hood, a spontaneous combustion in the trunk, sudden halts at cow crossings, and chicken barricades with feathers flying. There was even a rumor floating about: "One of those Morris boys got his gearshift stuck in reverse up at the schoolhouse and actually backed that big, awful car all the way up South Ridge Avenue—and with all those children inside it." Some folks carried the rumor even further: "All those children were hanging out the windows, hailing and directing the backward haul home."

TWELVE
Visiting Mama

OUR first long trip in the army tank was to visit Mama at the hospital, which was near the mountains and several hours away. I wanted to see Mama, but I didn't care much for seeing the hospital.

When we arrived at the gates, I sank into depression. A stone wall surrounded the grounds and all the hospital windows had heavy, black bars crisscrossing them from top to bottom. I searched for a window which wasn't barred and found none. *This seems more like a prison than a hospital,* I thought. The building was huge and massive—many stories high. Aged and cracking brick told me it had stood for many years. Ivy had overtaken parts of it, and it looked like an old haunted castle.

Dan parked the car and pointed to a park bench on the hospital grounds. "Wait for me over there," he said. The bench was guarded by a twisted oak which had to be older than the hospital. It bent to shade a large area around the cement bench. If only it could speak and tell of those who had come and gone from the hospital through the years. How many families, just like ours, had waited beneath the tree, anticipating the sight of their loved ones who had come as patients to this dismal place.

Soon Dan appeared and said that he had talked to a doctor who said that Mama would be coming out shortly to see us. My mind wilted into blankness until I saw a nurse dressed all in white coming toward us. Beside her was Mama.

Lillian and Jake jumped up and down. "Here she comes!" they squealed. "Here comes Mama!" They raced to embrace her, and Hank and Elizabeth hurried after them. I did the same. Mama bent down to kiss the little ones. She raised her head to smile through tear-filled eyes.

Hank changed the mood of things immediately. He gave Mama a big bear hug and turned the painful scene into one you might see at a church picnic. Hank knew how to make every situation a happy one, no matter what state of gloom hovered over it. I hugged Mama and smiled tearfully. "Hello, Melanie," Mama said, softly. "How's my blonde-haired girl?"

"I'm fine, Mama, just fine," I answered, overcome with joy at seeing Mama after such a long time. She looked so tall and restrained. I wished at that moment that I

Mama being hugged

could walk inside her heart and mend its broken parts.

Dan waited under the tree for us to join him there. Reunions were difficult occasions for Dan. He guarded his emotions and watched his words with great care on every occasion. When Mama approached, he hugged her gently. "Hello, Mama," he said.

"I'm so glad you're home, Dan!" Mama said.

Jake and Lillian had many things to say to Mama—all at the same time. Mama listened patiently, just as she'd always done, and passed generously warm glances to all of us. The white-clad nurse stood very close by and blessed our reunion with her smiles.

"When are you comin' home, Mama?" Lillian asked sweetly.

Mama lowered her head a moment. Then she spoke, "I don't know yet, Lillian, but let's all think that it will be soon—very soon."

"That's what we've always done, Mama, right from the start," Hank said joyfully.

"That's good," Mama answered. "It's the only way to think, son."

"Mama," Jake said, "ummm, where's the bathroom? I gotta go to the latrine."

"I'll show you where it is, little man," the nurse in white said, laughing. "Just come with me."

Jake followed the nurse toward the hospital entrance. "Hey, wait. I have to go, too," I fibbed and ran up the hill after them.

It was a long way to the front door. Climbing the hill, I gazed at all the barred windows and hoped to find a single window free of bars, but none was to be found. Bars meant only one thing to me: jail, imprisonment. I thought of what the kids at school jokingly said about a hospital like this. They had called it "the funny farm, the nut house, where crazy people end up and the 'men in little white jackets' come to carry you there." That's not how Mama had come here. She had come willingly and peacefully.

The nurse guided Jake and me into the hospital entrance hall. The hospital smelled sickeningly of medicine and anesthesia. The nurse directed Jake to the bathroom, and I wandered aimlessly into the waiting room.

It was dark and barren, musty and cold like a forbidden cave. The bars on the windows haunted me. I had to get away from the nurse in white. I dreamed of a new white dress someday, but not the kind she was wearing. I followed the direction Jake had taken, thinking the ladies room had to be nearby. I found a heavy door which I hurried through and then bumped my nose on the way. Once inside, I noticed the fixtures weren't the same. I held my aching nose. A stall door flew open, and Jake's mouth fell open as the john flushed.

"You're in the wrong room!" he said in a panicked voice. "You'd better get outta here before somebody sees you."

"I know, I know," I said painfully and bumped my nose again on the way out.

I'd missed the ladies room by one door.
Once safe inside it, I was all alone—at
last. I threw my arms nearly around a
stall door and wept on its cold wooden
chest. All the tears I'd held for weeks and
months came gushing forth.

I looked at the fluorescent light in the
ceiling. It was the only thing standing
between me and heaven. I beat my fists on
the stall door and spoke bravely toward
the light in the ceiling: "If you're up there,
behind that light bulb, then I know you
can hear me, and I know you're up there,
too. First it was Daddy," I sobbed. "Now
my mother is in—in jail. What's going to
happen next?"

I waited for an answer, but there was
only an eerie silence. "Well," I said,
waiting. Still, no answer, only a slight
flicker from the fluorescent light above.
"Then, I have to tell you just one thing,
and it's all I'm going to say: 'We're not
licked, yet.' None of us are. You'll see. . . .
I'm just mad enough to lick this world by
myself if I have to!"

I left the lonely room which had
rendered me so much relief—not the kind
it was intended for, but the kind I needed
at the time. I expected great bolts of
lightning to come down from heaven and
strike me dead the moment I walked
outside, but only sunshine and fresh air
struck me full in the face and warmed my
whole being. There wasn't a cloud in
sight.

Jake ribbed me about hitting the wrong
privy. "How many doors did you bump

into before you hit the right one? And what took you so long?"

"Are you all right, young lady?" the nurse asked.

"Yes, Ma'am, just something in my eye and a little headache and a toothache, too." I clenched my teeth, pointing to my eye, my head, and my mouth.

I'd never had a toothache in my life. Jake was my only headache now, and the red in my eyes came from aches of the spirit. The nurse looked at me with such pity that I couldn't stand it. I promised I'd never again have so many aches and pains of the spirit. I must have been a wretched sight. My inner stresses had shown through for the last time.

If an oyster can take an irritation and turn it into a pearl, Jake's effect on me was bound to change both of us into solid angels someday, complete with wire wings and tinselled halos—maybe we'd even change into real ones if we learned to take pain as the oysters did. Wonders never cease. I think I believed in miracles again.

I didn't resent the nurse taking Mama away. Suddenly I was fourteen and a half. I kissed Mama good-bye without a single tear.

THIRTEEN
Tombstones, Cows, and Epitaphs

DAN announced on the way home that we could visit Mama every two weeks as long as the car held out to carry us there. The trip to the hospital seemed much longer than the trip back home.

Lillian and Jake broke the monotony of the long ride home by playing a game called "Counting Cows," or "Cow Poker," as Jake called it. She counted all the cows on one side of the road, while he counted all the cows on the other side. The object of the game was to see who could count a hundred moo-cows first. A white horse was counted as five whole cows. We passed dozens of pastures where the contented animals grazed in abundance.

"I've got fifty-five cows, Lillian," Jake said. "How many do you have?"

"You don't have fifty-five cows for long," Dan said, "'cause up ahead is a graveyard on your side of the road, Jake. And that means you have to bury all your cows and start all over again."

"Oh, no!" Jake cried. "Spare me."

"Looks like we have another buryin' comin' up. I see a church steeple stickin' up on Lil's side of the road, now," Dan said.

Both Lillian and Jake mourned for their cows while Hank sang one of his favorite hymns, "Little Brown Church in the Dale," as a benediction to the cows passing. He sang it each time someone buried a cow.

Next to every cemetery we passed stood a little church, and I took notice of all the steeples. They stood tall and proud against the sky—in the cold of winter and the heat of summer. They looked the same on even the darkest night. Steeples were symbols of many good things—courage and strength. They also housed the church bells, and mama birds could nest in them in summer. How often I wished for the solitude of a single steeple. They made me think of the pointed belfries like the ones you see on castles in all the fairy tales.

Lillian won the "Cow Poker" game after we passed a barnyard where a half-dozen white horses grazed. It carried her score way over the winning mark, and the game was over. It was a good thing, too, because up ahead was another burying ground and it was on her side. "Saved by six white horses!" she cried.

When we approached the cemetery, Dan turned the car onto a little dirt road which ran beside it. The road looked familiar. "Why, this is my daddy's graveyard!" Lillian shouted.

The narrow dirt road led us to the side of the monument that had our family name on it. Daddy had put great stock in family names. He often said, "Folks should be proud of their name and their heritage."

We all got out and stood by the monument. Lillian ran to a vacant plot nearby and gathered all the wild purple irises she could find. She laid them on the green earth that covered Daddy. I sat down on the base of the granite tombstone which gave Daddy's name, his birthdate, and the date of death—a span of fifty years. I and the tombstone shared the same gray mood.

It was quiet and peaceful where Daddy rested. The sweet smell of spring drifted upward from Lillian's bouquet. I gave all the reverence I had to the moments I sat near Daddy's grave and to the thought of spring—the time of rebirth and new life bursting forth.

A honeybee lit on Lillian's wild irises and moved from flower to flower. Daddy had said that honeybees were God's greatest wonder. He had kept thousands of bees in snow-white beehives at Piedmont Apiaries, a big field next to our house. They used to get into our hair and sting our toes. But Daddy had said honeybees die when they lose their stingers. Whenever someone got stung, it meant that a honeybee died.

Lillian watched the honeybee until it flew away. Then other parts of the cemetery seemed to call her. She disappeared behind some tombstones. "Oh, come look, everybody!" she called. "This grave marker has a man's picture on it." We all followed her voice to the weathered picture on the tombstone and found others like it as we wandered through the graveyard. The mystery of it all lured us to discover the message on every tombstone. Hank read each verse aloud to Lillian who was especially taken by the ones inscribed on the tombstones of little children. She had to know exactly how old they had all been when they had died, both the young and the old. I wondered how they had died, what they had done in life, and what they had looked like, including what their eye color had been.

Before we could get lost deep in the cemetery, Dan signaled that it was time to leave. He whistled and pointed to the clock on his arm. Everyone headed for the car, except for Jake, who had to be whistled for again. We all fell into melancholy silence during the final moments by Daddy's grave. We drove away quietly with all heads turned to watch our family monument until it was out of sight.

Finally Lillian spoke, "When tombstones have verses on them, why are they so sad? Why don't they say something real about the person they're written for?"

"Yes," Elizabeth agreed. "Something to let you know that the person was once very real."

"Yeah," added Jake. "Why don't they tell things like what the person did for fun or even the funniest thing that ever happened to him? I bet everybody buried back there

had a real good time at least once in his life. I don't seee how they could all be saints—right off the bat. The ones with verses could at least tell how come they died. I want all those things on my tombstone," Jake announced.

"You want one that people will come back twice to read and bring somebody with them the second time, don't you, Jake?" Hank said. "I'll come up with one that will make you a legend, Jake."

Hank thought for a moment and then said:

Resting here is good ole Jake.
Got lost in the middle of Frog Pond Lake.
They say he sailed on a cardboard raft,
And disappeared with a hearty laugh.
Now his life is over and done,
But he died from having too much fun.

Everybody got a good laugh from Jake's epitaph, even Dan. Lillian laughed so hard she almost lost her breath, and Jake slapped her on the back. "What are you laughing for, Lil? You're next."

Jake racked his brain and then came up with a verse for her. "I got it," Jake said. "Somebody write this one down for Lil."

"I can't do it," I said. "I get carsick if I write or read while the car is moving."

Hank fumbled in the glove compartment for some paper and a pen and told Jake to start reciting. Jake began:

"Come look, everybody. . . . This grave marker has a man's picture on it!"

Lyin' here is Lillian Q.
Got a tack stuck in her shoe.
Worked its way plum through her sock.
Now she'll lie here 'til she rots.

Lillian put a frown on her smile just like
Dan, and I shrieked, "Jake, that's horrible!
How can you say that about Lillian—that
she's going to rot?"

"Well, that's what happens when people
die, Melanie. Right off, the rottin' sets in,"
Jake said.

I put my hands over my ears. "Don't
say that!" I shrieked. "I hate that word! It
sounds *awful.*"

Hank laughed. "Jake's right, you know.
That's even what the Good Book says,
Ashes to ashes and dust to dust."

"Melanie don't—doesn't want to believe
it," Jake said. "Ashes to ashes and dust to
dusty, but good ole Mel thinks you just get
rusty."

"That sounds better than the other word
you used that starts with an *r*," I said.

"You mean *rot*?" Jake asked, leaning
closer to me.

"Don't say that," I shuddered, holding
my ears. "It's worse than hearing chalk
squeak on a blackboard."

"There's a word that sounds much
better, Jake. Try using *rigamortasis*,"
Hank said.

"But that means 'to turn cold and stiff,'
doesn't it?" Elizabeth asked.

"Oh, Lordy!" I cried. "Please let's talk of
other things."

"But we haven't made up everybody's

epitaph yet," Hank said. "We've got to have one for everybody."

"OK," I said, "but you can leave mine out. I'm not ready for the obituaries *yet*."

As it turned out, Hank was the family poet. He scribbled out a verse for everyone else, except for him and me, and called his rhymes "The Tombstone Column." Then he read them aloud to us:

Here lies Dan, the army man.
Cut his finger on an ole tin can.
His finger took sick the very next day.
Now ole Dan's here wastin' away.

Buried here is Elizabeth Lee.
We found her under the apple tree.
She made no bets and owed no debts,
But left this world with one regret:
The poor ole girl ain't married yet.

"What about you, Hank? Where's your epitaph?" I asked.

"Why don't you make one up for me, Mel? I'm too modest to make up my own. Anyway, you're a pretty good poet from what I've read!" Hank replied.

"All right," I said. "You asked for it."

A lyin' here is good ole Hank.
Got hit in the head with a flyin' plank.
They say it fell right outta the sky,
And he passed away with a final sigh.
But he opened his eyes for one last word,
Which all the world around him heard:
"I know you'll miss me when I'm gone,
And mourn for me in every song—
And when a hundred years have flown,
I know my name will still be known."

By this time we were only a few miles from home. Hank said, "It's really not fair that everyone has a final eulogy but Melanie."

"Oh, yes, it is," I said. "I don't mind at all."

"I've thought of one for you, Melanie," Elizabeth said. "Don't you want to hear it?"

"Oh, all right. I'd rather you'd say my rites than anybody, Liz."

"Here goes, Melanie."

Here is resting Melanie Kay.
Bumped her nose three times a day,
Laughed and cried wherever she went.
Now her life has all been spent.
Near her is a rising steeple,
Faraway from all the people.
This is what she liked the best,
'Til she drew her final breath.

I sat in awe over Elizabeth's verse, although it drew some laughs from the crowd. How did she know I'd bumped my nose? I suppose Jake, the informer, had told her, but nobody, except my diary, knew I liked steeples.

Elizabeth would never pry into someone's diary, but Jake would, if he could find the key. I doubted it. I had a good hiding place now. But had he? No, I could tell when Jake was guilty, and he didn't have that look on his face. Elizabeth's magic powers were just one more of her special gifts.

FOURTEEN
Stubborn Troopers

"JAKE, it's time for that haircut you've been needing," Hank said one Saturday morning. "I'm going to take you to that new barber uptown. Here's a dollar-and-a-half to cover it."

"Can I keep the change?" Jake asked.

"There won't be any change. It'll take every penny to pay for your cut," Hank answered.

"But what if there *is* some change?" Jake asked.

"Then you can keep it, I guess. OK, let's see how fast you can get into the car."

They headed toward town, and Hank commented, "I can't believe you're going so willingly, Jake, without a fight and all."

"I'm not. Stop here, Hank, or I'll—I'll throw a fit or throw myself out of the car, maybe."

"Good heavens, all right. What do you want to stop here for? This is Mr. Nelms' house," Hank said, turning into the drive.

"I know," Jake answered. "I'm going to get one of Mr. Nelms' haircuts."

"You're not!" Hank said, bewildered. "Not a Nelms' Special? You really don't mean that, Jake. What can I do to change your mind?"

"Nothin'," Jake answered. "I'll be savin' a dollar-and-a-quarter. Who can beat a haircut for twenty-five cents?"

"A sheep shearer," Hank said.

Mr. Nelms had been Daddy's cohort in beekeeping. A sign in his front yard said:

Honey—$1.25 a quart——Sourwood Honey— $1.50

Mr. Nelms didn't advertise the haircuts he gave in his front parlor. The haircuts he gave were the military kind where you have no hair left when it's over. He'd been the official barber aboard a naval ship when he was a young sailor.

"You aren't going to try and stop me now, are you, Hank?" Jake asked, as they walked up to the door.

"Oh, no, I wouldn't do that. After all, Dan and I both had one of those haircuts once. I wouldn't want to deprive you of one. I'm just glad Mama's not here to see it, that's all. She almost never recovered from mine and Dan's haircuts."

"Well, I wouldn't do it if I wern't savin' so much money," Jake said.

"Suit yourself," Hank sighed. "It's your head, and it's a stubborn one. Daddy was right when he said all his children were bullheaded and longheaded."

"Well, howdy, boys. What can I do for you?" Mr. Nelms said, chewing the end of a big black cigar.

"Jake wants a haircut, Mr. Nelms," Hank said.

"Well, does he now? Why that won't take but a minute. Hop right up here, boy. Now you're right sure you want one of these haircuts?" he said, getting out his equipment.

"Yes, sir," Jake answered, swallowing bravely.

The clippers zipped across Jake's crop of hair, which landed in big hunks on the floor. "Guess a body hadn't lived 'til it's had one a *my* haircuts," Mr. Nelms said proudly.

Mr. Nelms shaved his own head straight up on both sides, and what was left on top stood straight up in the air. He may have used beeswax to help it along. Something sure made it stand up tall.

Mr. Nelms missed Daddy as much as anybody. They and some other friends of theirs had started the County Beekeeper's Association. Daddy had been one of its earlier presidents. He'd also served as state president one year. According to Daddy, Mr. Nelms, and their associates, honey cured all ills, and beeswax did almost the same.

Jake had little to say on the way home. He sat with his new GI haircut opposite Hank and counted his money.

"You've become a typical, old pinch-penny miser, Jake, complete with bald head and all. I don't suppose you'd tell me

141

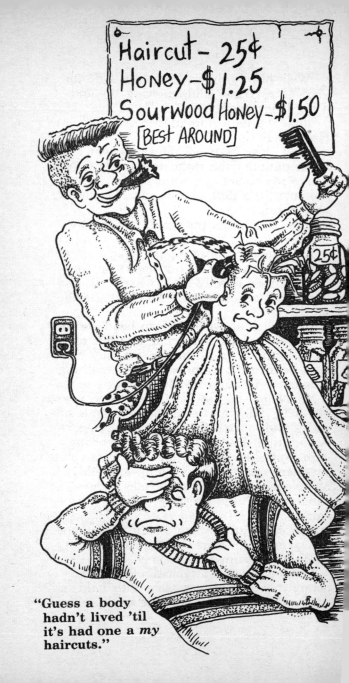

"Guess a body hadn't lived 'til it's had one a *my* haircuts."

what you're saving all your money for, would you?"

"Nope, I'm not tellin' a livin' soul," Jake said.

"And I don't suppose you know anything either about who's been donating Monopoly money in the church offering plate on Sundays lately and signing the name *unanimus* to the tithing envelope because they can't spell *anonymous*? I only know of one person who spells that bad."

"Don't know a thing about it," Jake said, still counting his change.

Hank dropped the subject to think of other important matters, but Jake had us all stumped on his money matters.

Hank had the junior-senior prom to think about that night. He stood in front of the mirror, admiring himself for hours. We begged him to tell us whom he was taking to the prom.

"Sally McQuarter," he'd say, each time we asked him.

Both Dan and Hank referred to all amiable girls as "Sally McQuarter," but there was no such person that we knew of.

"Come on, Hank! Tell us," we pleaded. "Dan calls all pretty girls 'Sally McQuarter,' so she's his girl, not yours."

"I'm taking the loveliest, most sought-after creature in school. That's who," Hank answered.

"Who could that be?" we asked.

"Oh, just sweet little Sally McQuarter," he said, pinching Lillian on the cheek.

We were so annoyed by Hank's

stubbornness that we wished him all kinds of ill fate.

Jake wished that Hank would flush Sally's corsage down the toilet by mistake.

Elizabeth wished four flat tires on old Tin Lizzy Lee right in front of Sally Whoever's house.

Lillian said, "Maybe the ole tank won't even start, because maybe she'll be jealous."

And I hoped Sally wouldn't even be at home when Hank got there.

"You're all acting like you've suddenly become malicious menaces to the human race," Hank said, splashing Dan's after-shave all over his head.

Elizabeth wrote down the words Hank had used to describe us, so she could look them up in the dictionary after he left, even though she already had a pretty good idea what they all meant. It was common for Hank to use big words on us!

Hank smiled one last time into the mirror, patted his hair, reared back, and with corsage in hand, marched out to the old tin tank.

Just as Elizabeth was about to release all the information she'd gathered from the dictionary, the back door flung open. Hank stood there with sweat dripping off his brow. "Where's Dan?" he asked, out of breath.

"Polishing his army boots," Elizabeth answered, "but we thought you left twenty minutes ago to pick up Sally McQuarter."

Hank took off through the house. In no time, he and Dan bounded down the back steps toward the stubborn tank. A half hour later Dan walked into the house, wiping grease and oil from his hands. Hank followed after him with his tuxedo jacket slung over his shoulder and his shirt-sleeves rolled up above his elbows.

"This time, she has to have a new battery," Dan said. "If I call the garage, it'll take maybe two hours or more. That car's just ornery, I reckon. We never know what she's gonna do. She'll be needin' some new tars on the back soon, too."

Hank took a deep breath, rolled his eyes toward the ceiling, and then fixed them hard on me, Elizabeth, Jake, and Lillian, who all felt a bit sick now and awfully sorry for our wicked wishing.

"How does it feel to be four practicing wizards whose magic works?" Hank asked us.

"Awh, you know we didn't mean all those things," Jake said, slapping Hank on the back.

"It makes me feel awful," Lillian said, almost weeping.

"But Hank, you called us. . . ."

"Never mind what he called us, Elizabeth," I interrupted. "Ummm, what happened, Hank?"

"Just about everything you all wished would happen," Hank said, moping into the kitchen.

Hank closed the door. We could hear him dialing the phone and then mumbling something into the receiver. Jake stuck his ear to the door, but had no luck hearing what Hank was saying.

In a few moments Hank opened the door and plopped down into a chair. "Phew," he sighed. "I should just turn all of you into polecats, but on the other hand, anyone for a game of Monopoly?"

The four of us wayward wonder-workers sat down, hung our heads, and felt like pure "dawgs."

Jake and I got out the Monopoly game while Hank changed from his tuxedo. Elizabeth and Lillian gathered all our schoolbooks from off the study table.

"Melanie," Jake said in a joking tone, "have you heard anythin' about one of our church members donatin' phony money to the church?"

"Heavens, no, Jake! Why would anyone do a crazy thing like that?"

"Maybe he needed the real money for somethin' he thought was more important at the time."

"Nobody at our church is that stingy," I said laughing. "Unless," I swallowed hard. "Jake, is this Monopoly game missing some phony bills?"

Jake shook his head yes. "I put a couple in church, not all on the same Sunday, though. Just one at a time."

"Oh, Lord, have mercy!" I moaned, dropping half the game on the floor. I sank into a chair and held my head. "*Why*, Jake? Why did you do a thing like that? Dan gives us all tithe money each Sunday. Why did you keep yours? Are you in trouble?" I was half sick and the most mad I'd ever been at Jake. I could just hear Miz Alexandria saying, "Ah told you so. Ah knew one of them was gonna 'go to the bad.'"

"No, I'm not in trouble. I've been savin' my money to buy somethin' nice for Mama. I didn't think the good Lord would mind. Least my envelope wasn't empty."

"Oh, Jake, I suppose the Lord understands your reason for skimpin' on him, but please put your church money in church from now on."

"I will," Jake said, "but how will I get enough money to buy somethin' nice for Mama?"

"I've got a little money. I'm sure everybody else has a little, too. It won't be much, but we can put it all together—like we do to buy gas. We'll come up with enough. It'll just take time."

"Please don't tell Hank or Dan what I did."

"I won't, Jake. Isn't that why you had your head scalped—and it's now under that baseball cap you're wearing—to save money?"

Jake shook his head yes.

I felt like a pure "dawg" all over again, but this time I wished I were an old dead one in the middle of the road—with its feet sticking straight up in the air from that awful "rigamortasis."

Jake and I did not like discussing money, whether it was a little or a lot. As far as we were concerned, money was a necessary evil. I believe all of us had the same opinion: if every success story on earth were linked with the love of money alone, then no one at our house would ever

have a success story to tell. There had to be a better motive than simply acquiring money!

We'd hardly started the Monopoly game when someone pounded hard on the front door.

"I'll get it," Hank said, "but don't anybody move 'til I buy the deed to Park Place."

A tough-looking man in a uniform stood at the front door. "Your name *Hank?*" he asked.

"Yes, sir," Hank answered, gulping.

"Good. Your taxi's here," he said.

"But I—I didn't call for a—a taxi," Hank stammered.

"Look, buddy, all I know is that a young lady called for a taxi to come to this address to pick up a guy named Hank— and you're him, ain't you?"

"Well, yes, sir, but gimme five minutes."

Hank shrugged his shoulders at us as if he were baffled and disappeared into his room. Five minutes later he closed the front door, leaving with corsage in one hand and tuxedo jacket in the other.

"Good-bye, you all," he said, grinning. "You can sell Park Place to the highest bidder." He winked and was gone.

Elizabeth, Jake, Lillian, and I sat shaking our heads. There was nothing left to say but "Sally McQuarter."

Elizabeth got the last word in. "I told you Hank always comes out smelling like a rose."

FIFTEEN
Spring Goes Marching On

SPRING was my favorite time of year. Maybe it was for all of us. We soon began counting the days until school would be over, but the whooping and hollering which ushered in the days of summer was just getting started.

We celebrated Hank's birthday on May 24th. Everybody wore those funny little hats that looked like steeples with ruffles around the bottom. Hank's vocal "chimes" had been ringing for about a week before the party to remind us that "the most important day in all of history was just around the corner." Elizabeth baked the cake to make sure that no fireworks went off in the oven before the party started, but Jake told someone that I was the last person seen stirring the cake batter before it went into the oven.

Dan did not let spring begin to fade out without reminding us that even though "R and *R*" (*Rest* and *Recreation*) was on its way, we still had to maintain the fort in our regular line of duty. He said we might be allowed to go to bed at 10:00 P.M. instead of at 9:30 P.M., but we would have to rise and shine just the same. After all, we'd all have plenty of time to sleep when we "got to our graves." Dan believed that no one should sleep after the sun rose or stay awake long after it set.

Dogwood winter and blackberry winter, the last two cold snaps of spring, signaled that some long, hot days were on their way. The effect of school on my spring fever was a terrible burden. I'd rather have been singing or dreaming or floating through a field of crocus blossoms than having to concentrate on coming exams, reports, or IQ tests. It had to be an awful sin to let spring pass by without our absorbing it—like eating lemon pie without even tasting it.

I suffered myself to endure some "comprehension tests," which were the same as IQ measurement tests to show how much our intellects had improved during the course of the year. But since my mind was so agonized at the thought of missing spring, my test scores agonized, too. I can't blame spring alone for my intelligence score indicating a borderline blooming idiot. Standardized tests of any sort left me bewildered, much the way I left my tireless math teacher. I just couldn't comprehend "those kinds of tests" at all, although I did think they were maybe good for some people and had their place in the realm of conventional learning. I guess I was using a different yardstick for measuring how smart a person is.

Needless to say, the permanent score that went down on my record caused Dan to come down on me hard—with one of his sermons. He said, "Because of that awful score, do you realize, Melanie, that you may never ever, in your whole life put together, find a decent job!" Oh, after his words I wished I were a flower blowing in the wind.

There was no use in telling our "sarg" that I'd been thinking of the flowers outside. When Dan thought of flowers, he thought of funerals, too. Everything was so "grave" to Dan. I often prayed that heaven would send him some of the good Lord's humor.

Leave it to Dan to balance my dreamings. He was right, though. He always was. There was a season for everything: tears, laughter, dreams, and seriousness. Dan taught us all to endure the responsibilities of each season, and most of all, he taught us to see "reality," that overrated word.

After Dan's sermon in memory of my test score, I saw myself ten years later sitting in the personnel department of a wood-pulp-and-sawdust factory. The personnel director would look at my resumé, my references from kind people and then my IQ score. Then looking at me, he'd say, "I'm sorry, Miss—um—."

"Melanie," I'd say. "just plain Melanie."

"Miss Melanie," the distressed man would continue," we don't have a thing right now. We had an opening last week on the third-shift maintenance crew, but I've been told that an enterprising, young college student, who's working his way through school, is eagerly taking that position. Come back and see us when you have more experience. . . ."

The next thing I imagined was my IQ score etched out on a grave marker and on my social security card. Oh, horrors. Then I viewed myself walking with a tattered, old suitcase in hand and heading straight for a door in the distance marked "Poorhouse." Fear sparked me to never ever make the same mistake again!

My next calamity was an historical character report on someone who was either very famous or not so famous and had made a contribution to mankind and to our country. That was hard. First of all, I'd never known any famous people, and second of all, the report was due before the end of school and was to be given orally. Reciting in public was my Achilles' heel— my downfall. It gave me hot and cold sweats, instant ulcers, strange twitches, and shaky joints, weeks ahead of time.

A dread affliction would strike me just before I stood to speak in public. It never failed. Moments prior to my speaking, I'd always see my whole life flash before me, just as I'd heard about drowning victims seeing their entire lives before them as they were going down for the last time. I can't convey how terribly irksome that was.

To make matters worse, what always flashed before me were all the "mean" things I'd ever done in my life. The first thing was when I trimmed Elizabeth's eyelashes with the sewing shears out of pure jealousy because everyone said hers were pretty and never said a word about mine. That was the last time that I, or anyone else, ever talked Elizabeth into anything. I ate "humble pie" a long time after that deed—until Elizabeth's lashes grew back twice as long, and have remained so to this day. Oh, I hoped it wouldn't be carved on my tombstone—that mean, wicked thing I'd done to my sister.

The next exploit I could never escape reviewing was the time I "tested" some of Aunt Desma's expensive "Chanel No. 5 perfume" from right out of her pocketbook. It was just sitting there, peeping at me from the top of Aunt Desma's handbag perched on the coffee table. *It won't hurt to try a dab*, I thought. *Just a little dab.* So, I put a dab here and there and everywhere, while Mama and Aunt Desma chatted in the kitchen. All those dabs never produced the essence of Chanel No. 5 one iota. I later learned that it wasn't high-priced perfume I'd splashed on at all, but instead, a specimen which Aunt Desma had planned on presenting to her kidney specialist. Oh, what luck and what dreadful retribution to pay for such a small, pilfering sin! Besides, Jake, the informer, spread the word for the next six months as if he had been ordained to do so! Hank said he didn't think that washing seven times in the river Jordan would take that "perfume specimen" off me. Aunt Desma was much kinder. She never told those ladies she worked with at the Baptist Bookstore what I'd done. She didn't have to. Jake got to them first.

My guilt-ridden soul next reviewed the twenty-two flower pots I'd dumped on the floor because I thought my Aunt Inez, the dear soul who'd named me at birth, had gone off and left me alone in the house. She was just potting more plants out in the yard, while I was inside with my fears running wild.

Then I saw myself roller-skating all over Grandma's shiny hardwood floor in her living room. I was pretending to be an illustrious ice skater entertaining a grand audience. Grandma never made people pay for their sins. She only said, "Those old floors can be restored, but I can't. . . . They'll be here long after I'm gone, so you can skate all you want to for as long as I live."

My biographical list of sins could go on and on, but there was still the history report to deliver, and the results of it aged me a decade. Sympathetic to the cause, Hank approved my choice of a great person to report on. He said he couldn't have made a better choice himself. I chose someone who was very great in my and Hank's eyes.

We had all the colorful facts firsthand,

which could not be obtained from any written books to date. Hank offered a complete log of information for my character sketch, as though he were a walking journal. When I asked him if he had any impressive words to describe our hero, he rattled off half the dictionary. The only word I understood out of the whole lot was *genius*, so I stuck to my own adjectives.

The eventful day for my history report grew nearer, and the night before, I tried twisting my hair up in the latest style. I'd recently learned a new curling method from a friend, or at least I thought she was my friend until I decided to sleep on the method. I could have weathered it if I hadn't had that history report to sleep on, too. Both of them at the same time were too much. In the middle of the night I released my poor head from the torture of wire balloon curlers with brushes inside them and a special kind of stickpin to keep them from falling down. Sleep was hard enough without sticking wires and pins through my head.

The next morning it was raining, so Elizabeth, Lillian, and I stepped into the Sunday dusters we were also using as raincoats. The ornate flap at the waist on the back of my duster was coming loose. Elizabeth hurriedly sewed my flap back on with green thread while we were in the car on the way to school. She sewed the flap back to my duster, but also accidentally sewed it to all the layers of clothes underneath! So, when I stood, my coat was permanently hiked way up in the back to a point somewhere between my shoulder blades and my waistline. I was stuck for the rest of the day or else had to cry for help—which I wasn't about to do.

In class I sat with cold, wet hands and my back next to the wall. I was dreading that awful moment of the drowning flashes, which I felt approaching. I sized up the class and thought about who was going to benefit from my chronological notes.

In front of me was Bonnie Noland, whose long silky hair I coveted. Sitting in front of Bonnie was the prettiest girl in school. Beside me sat the smartest girl in school—my best friend since the first grade. In front of her sat Mike, my most trusted friend of the opposite sex and the shortest boy in school. I always tried sitting while talking to Mike so I wouldn't have to look down at him, but I had the feeling he'd outgrow us all someday. Then there was Junior Barnes, who had, for a time, lived in the middle of a country club golf course near some burial grounds until the country club moved to higher ground and a new shopping mall took its place. I often wondered what Junior's life had been like on a golf course because I couldn't see that Junior cared one smidgeon for golf.

In the last seat on the last row sat Big Red, the most red-headed, freckled boy within a twenty-mile radius. Everybody was fond of likable Big Red despite his freckles. I imagined Big Red would be close to dying when he heard my narration. I knew he didn't care much for the kind of character I was reporting on. Big Red liked sports and probably that was all. I figured he'd be reporting on the man who invented baseball since someone said in class that the same man had fired the first cannonball during the Civil War and it was the shot that started the war.

Everybody was reporting on people like Abe Lincoln, Benjamin Franklin, Betsy Ross—those well-known figures you read about in books. The closer my turn came, the sicker I felt.

The drowning flashes of my past bad deeds began closing in on me, too: cutting Elizabeth's eyelashes off at the roots, snitching Aunt Desma's "perfume" specimen, dumping the twenty-two flower pots, "ice skating" on Grandma's shiny hardwood floors, and one I'd almost forgotten—causing Hank's birthday cake to explode in the oven because I was certain that one *extra* big dash of baking soda was just what it needed. The house smelled for weeks after the explosion!

There was no getting around it. The flashes accompanied all of my public speeches, as if speeches were my execution.

SIXTEEN
A Trooper Tale
or Two

WHEN Miss Preston, my history teacher, said it was my turn to address the class, I walked weak-kneed toward the front, praying that no one would notice how my coat was hiked way up in the back and that the good Lord would forgive me for all my abominations.

My shaky voice began: "The historical figure I've chosen to report on cannot be found in any history book, nor in any encyclopedia—neither the *World Book* nor the *Britannica*—nor in Mr. Webster's dictionary. But the information I've gathered has come to me firsthand, mostly from the person himself and from stories handed down about him, rather than from books." I looked at Miss Preston, who nodded and said, "Go on, Melanie."

The whole class was awaiting my revelation, so I went on. "This man was a great humanitarian, a statesman, a humorist, and an ecclesiastical legend in his own time. His goal in life was to establish churches, to spread the gospel, and to bring poor lost sinners into the church's fold."

At the words "poor lost sinners," I thought Big Red was going to jump out the window. He squirmed at his desk and dove, more red-faced than he usually was, for the glass casement next to him and created a big commotion in the rear of the room. Miss Preston's head darted up, "What's going on back there?" she called out.

Big Red threw up the window, almost sending it through the roof. "I need some air, Miss Preston," he said, slumping back into his desk chair the way old people fall into a "sinking spell" or a "hot flash." He made a mouth that gave away his tortured state. His eyes seemed to be throwing darts at me, and they weren't the cupid kind. I was thankful that Big Red had put some fresh air into the room. I was about to faint in that heavy blue duster sewed to my clothes.

Miss Preston signaled for me to continue. "This profound man," I resumed, "contributed to the founding and building of over twenty-five Baptist churches during his lifetime. Some of the churches he served are only within a few miles of our county and community. The list includes Miami Church, Mount Pleasant. . . . However, no one knows the full extent of his work, but he became widely known as a great church-builder, and I am proud to say that this outstanding gentleman is my grandfather, the Reverend John Seamore Harris.

"He was born on December 5, 1878, on a farm in Oakboro, North Carolina. He received most of his formal education at the Baptist Theological Seminary in Kentucky and at Big Lick Academy near Red Cross, North Carolina, where he was ordained into the ministry. In the beginning, he traveled in a horse and buggy as a circuit preacher, and at one time he was a schoolteacher and was one of only two public instructors who served Stanly County during those days."

I went on with all the vital facts about Grandpa—how he and Grandma had raised fourteen children and how the children and Grandma had run the farm and worked the fields while Grandpa was out in the mission field for the gospel.

"He never ran for political office, but was a strong supporter of Christian leaders who served our government. We have a letter written to Grandpa personally from President Franklin Roosevelt asking Grandpa's opinion on an issue."

I closed my report with the humor in Grandpa's life. "Being a curious and adventurous man, Grandpa was keen on new inventions and was always one of the first to try the latest thing. He lived to see the invention of television, which he appreciated even more than the first Model T Ford. This 'new fangled gadget' allowed Grandpa to sit in on every political caucus, convention, and rally which was televised throughout the remainder of his days. Feeling as though he'd been transported to the scene of things by some kind of magic, Grandpa took part in every event he viewed. When someone on the television said, 'Turn out the light,' Grandpa got up and turned out the light.

"It was those western movies that turned Grandpa's nerves. Though he enjoyed them immensely, he couldn't stand all those horses and cows being in the house and kicking up so much dirt. They kept his TV-screen dusty! When Wild Bill Hickok and Andy Devine galloped across the screen, Grandpa dusted his set each time they passed through. He kept the same dustcloth handy for Roy Rogers, Gene Autry, Hopalong Cassidy, Gabby Hayes, Lash LaRue, and the Lone Ranger. . . ."

That evening during supper the whole homemade army wanted to know how my report on Grandpa had gone in school. Jake led the question-and-answer period.

"Did you tell about the time Grandpa ordered a Cheer wine soda in a restaurant up North and the waitress brought him real wine?" Jake asked. "Poor Grandpa. When he learned he'd drunk real wine, he asked the Lord to forgive him, for he had tasted the 'spirits of firewater' and didn't know what he was doing. You did tell that one on Grandpa, didn't you, Mellie?"

"No, I did not," I answered.

"That episode reminds me of the time Grandpa sinned on purpose," Hank remarked laughingly.

"How could he sin on purpose?"
Elizabeth asked. "That must be top-secret
information, but I don't believe it—not
Grandpa. What did he do?"

"It was top secret—released just last
summer by cousins Betty Jo, Jane, and
Kay, who are accessories to the fact and
are as guilty as Grandpa, if not more."

"Well, for goodness sake, Hank, tell us!
What did he do?" We wanted to know
before we all burst.

"He went to the circus and had more
fun than Betty Jo, Jane, and Kay ever
dreamed of having, but he made them
promise 'Never to tell,' because some of the
old folks in his congregation then thought
the circus was a den of iniquity—the very
idea of someone feeding monkeys and
talking to clowns! Anyone who did that
was headed straight for. . . ."

". . .Don't say that word at the supper
table!" Dan interrupted. "We know where
the devil's playground could send a
person."

"I wish I could have gone, too," Lillian
said, "but I wasn't borned yet!"

"You'd better be glad," Jake said, "or
you'd be headed straight for the same
place our three cousins are headed."

"Right! I'd be headed straight for the
circus with Grandpa if I could!" Lillian
said, still unable to connect the circus with
'that other place.'

"Did you tell about how Grandpa
proposed to Grandma and plucked all the
leaves off a crab apple tree—the one
Grandma was sittin' under for shade—

while he tried to get the words out?" Jake asked.

"No, I did not," I answered.

"Well, whad'ya tell about him? I bet you made Grandpa look like he wasn't genuwine—like one of those emortals who's never done nothin' human in his whole life," Jake said disgusted.

"No, I did not," I said to Jake for the last time.

"Did you say anything about his politics," Hank asked, "the way you planned?"

"Yes, I did. I told them Grandpa agreed with everything a man said as long as he believed in everything Grandpa believed in and thought the same thoughts Grandpa thought. Otherwise, John Harris took a stand that was cemented all the way to his grave."

The word *grave* brought a comment from Dan: "That's the gospel truth!"

The next day in school, it got back to me that someone said, "Sometimes her religion oozed out, spilled over, and dripped down over her." I didn't care a fairly-well-thank-you what that someone had said. I'd have made the same report all over again. Besides, I made an *A* for my efforts. And if anybody had trouble figuring out me and my efforts, that was *their* problem, not mine.

The ancient history report on Grandpa set off a whole new revival of old tales about him. He was the main hero of our tribal folklore, and I soon became the recorder of that grand family literature.

"Grandpa preached up a storm. . . ."

Hank said we should set it all down on paper for posterity's sake before we all became senile and forgot the stories. Our great grandchildren would get the stories straight as they really happened, instead of from aging imbeciles, which Hank predicted we were all bound to become should we live so long.

Recounting Grandpa's adventures often dissolved the boredom of many a long summer evening. Hank usually began by saying, "Remember the time Grandpa actually preached up a storm? Lightning flashed, thunder roared, and Grandpa spilled out his sermon while the rains poured. The rivers and streams overflowed, and water came clear up to the church steps that day. The congregation had to wade home or wait 'til the waters receded. Grandpa said he'd preached fire and brimstone before, but that was the first time he'd ever preached up a storm."

Then Dan told the story that cousin Otis told him once. On the way to church one Sunday, Otis asked Grandpa to "pleeze" stop preaching at twelve o'clock and let everybody go home because Grandma had something really good fixed for Sunday dinner that day. Grandpa promised to stop preaching as Otis had requested. When noon came, Grandpa promptly closed his sermon, but then he walked over to the old pump organ and began playing and singing and leading the congregation in one hymn after another. Grandpa played the pump organ until 12:30; then low and behold, picked up his fiddle and fiddled until 1:00. Otis was close to starvation by then, but Grandpa promised on the way home that Grandma's good cooking would make up for it all—which it did. Otis said, "Grandpa could play the strings off a fiddle and make a pump organ sing!"

One tall tale about Grandpa Harris called for another, and each was declared the absolute truth. Dan never closed his story-telling session without recalling what Mr. Hartsell down in Oakboro had told

Grandpa could play the
strings off a fiddle . . .

. . . and make the old
pump organ sing. . . .

him. It seems that Mr. Hartsell, Grandpa, and four other men went fox hunting one day with fourteen dogs. The dogs tracked down the prey, but no one could hear them barking. In fact, they didn't catch a single fox, because Grandpa talked above the voices of five men and the howling of fourteen dogs! Mr. Hartsell raises his right hand that what he told about Grandpa was the gospel truth.

Grandpa Harris always had crowds around him. We have pictures of him baptizing the multitudes in the river, while throngs of onlookers lined the riverbank with their Model T Fords all parked in the background. My memories of Grandpa were mostly of his visits to our house and his wearing his toboggan cap to bed. When he awakened at 5:30 A.M., he'd be ready to discuss his two favorite topics with Daddy—religion and politics. Grandpa's voice rose with him. In fact, it was the same in the early dawn as it was in the pulpit!

Since our house was small and voices carried, everybody heard Grandpa. Jake said that there had to be a switch somewhere that turned Grandpa off or one that at least turned his volumn down. Hank said that there wasn't one of either kind anywhere—only one turned Grandpa on and that was all!

Daddy never once let his father-in-law know that he was registered on the opposite political ticket from him. It was only to protect Grandpa and not shorten Grandpa's days.

Grandpa Harris was one of the few people besides us children who never seemed bothered by the trains which passed just beyond our backyard day and night. Everything quivered to the thunder of the trains, but it didn't trouble Grandpa or the rest of us.

People who came to visit during the day couldn't help notice the trains. They'd usually plug up their ears and make a comment or two: "How can you *stand* living here?" or "I hope you all got good foundations around here! Law, I'd move away from this place!" What really did people in were those night trains. As a result, overnight visitors rarely came back again unless they returned with earplugs and several sets of earmuffs!

One frazzled guest went away saying that every two hours during the night, a volcano rose up and erupted in our backyard. According to Hank, another guest, who was unaware of what "trains in the night" could do for him, was so terrified by all the thunder and rumbling that he woke up, thinking he was surely dying and on his way to that fiery furnace of flames which burn forever and ever. He jumped out of bed and fell to his knees. Hank looked down from his top bunk and said, "Hey, what are you doing down there?" The trembling voice from below answered, "I'm on my knees, Lord, but I wish I'd done it sooner, 'cause I don't want to die and burn forever." Hank was extremely flattered that his voice had been mistaken for a voice from heaven.

For some reason, most people's idea of a good night's rest did not include the nightmare of sleeping in beds which actually moved across the floor in a house which trembled every two hours during any given night. But Grandpa Harris was one big exception!

If there was another person who could endure as well as Grandpa did and had the same spirit of adventure, it was Mrs. Willis. She was the better half of our minister, the Reverend W. M. Willis, but they both had the same initials and first names, so people sometimes got confused and never knew who the Reverend was— he or she!

Just being near Mrs. Willis was like setting sail for new and unknown frontiers, especially if our daring brother, Hank, was also nearby. They both had something exciting up their sleeves almost all the time for the benefit of every young person in our church.

Thanks to Mrs. Willis' encouragement, I rose to the highest plateau in Girl's Auxiliary. Hank said he was certain the feat had raised my IQ considerably and that now I ranked with an Eagle Scout. I wondered if every triumphant scout memorized what I'd memorized to soar like an eagle.

Mrs. Willis took us to Ridgecrest, to Camp Caswell, and to every Baptist youth rally in the state. She truly loved young people and had a special gift which she used especially with the youth, whom she dealt with in great numbers. What she had was an exceptional way of making the young people in our church believe that they could do anything they wanted to with "mountains," for "mountains" were meant to be climbed and conquered. Mrs. Willis' philosophy went something like this: heroes are born every day, but it takes someone with great courage to stake his claim on the birthright.

Mrs. Willis said that I had an artistic gift and should pursue it. She said I got it from Mama, who could sit down at a piano or an organ and play every song in the old, green Broadman Hymnal without reading a note. The first time Mama heard "How Great Thou Art," she went straight to a piano and played it by heart. It became Mama's favorite hymn. Mama played mostly by ear—all Grandpa's children played instruments—and had a beautiful alto voice to go with it. Lillian had Mama's voice.

Mama also had other talents that people didn't know about. She used to make us the most beautiful little floral and gingham-print dresses out of empty flour sacks from Daddy's store. The flour came in sacks made from material bearing lovely designs, and Mama recycled them when all the flour was gone. A lady in our church once said to Mama, "Your children always look as though they just stepped out of a bandbox. They would all look fine though, even if you dressed them in 'toe sacks.'"

Mama just smiled and replied, "Yes, I guess they would," but she never told anyone it was "toe-sacks" we were wearing.

Mama had used her creative genius on many occasions, just as Mrs. Willis believed people should. Mrs. Willis said, "If you do not use it, you will be sure to lose it." She got me into the poster-making business, which she predicted would develop my artistic abilities. She believed in me and showed it. "No effort is ever a mistake, but a stepping-stone to the final goal," she'd say. Poster-making, a non-profit business in our church, promised rewards in later years. Those artistic attempts on my part were used as visual aids throughout our church, but Mrs. Willis saw them as little Rembrandts.

However, there was one poster in particular that neither she nor anybody else ever saw—only a few critics. It showed "Steeple Sam," actually Uncle Sam dressed up like a church with a fine steeple on his head. He was calling people into a church service. "Uncle Sam" had been inspired by Dan, the army man, and he was drawn perfectly on the poster. It was complete except for the words, *"THIS CHURCH WANTS YOU!"* When I called in the troops for a preview, I presented the poster the way all great works of art should be revealed—with an unveiling. They were impressed with the unveiling, but not with my poster!

"Well," I said confidently. "What do you think?"

For a few moments you could have heard a pin drop. Then they moved in

closer to get a better look. This time I had
them all stumped.

"Ummm, is that modern art?" Jake
asked.

"No," I said. "Now look closely. What do you think it is?"

"The wizard of Oz," Elizabeth said bluntly.

I looked carefully at my poster, turning it this way and that, and grimaced a bit. I used to think Liz had the gift of discernment. "Oh, Liz, do you honestly think that's what it looks like?"

"Well, yes, but it could be a Halloween goblin in a witch's hat, I guess. Then again, it could be a stool pigeon in a dunce cap. Which one is it?" Elizabeth remarked.

Elizabeth was sincere. That did it! The veil had been rent and I, torn asunder.

"It's neither!" I said to Elizabeth and turned to Lillian to ease the pain a bit. "What does it look like to you, Lil, honey?"

"Oh, it's a fat, jolly clown in a clown's hat or a birthday hat, maybe. Is that right, Melanie?"

"No, Lillian, honey, that's not right." I turned to my youngest brother. "Well, Jake, it's your turn again, so let's hear it, but step lightly, would you? I don't know if I can take it."

"Oh, I know exactly what it is! I've known all along. Anyone can plainly see that ole man's an ole mountaineer with his jug missing, but how come you got a lightnin' rod on the top of his hat?"

I closed my eyes and shook my head. I frowned. "How can anyone be so misunderstood? How, how, *how!* This is a *church* poster!"

Hank heard my despairing words and

interceded. "Now, now, Melanie, things are never as bad as you think they are. Cheer up. This poster could be used for something, I'm sure. I know! It would be a grand advertisement for the ten-cent Saturday noon matinee at the Swanee Theater uptown, when they feature Ma and Pa Kettle at an old-timey brush arbor church meeting."

"Never!" I said to Hank. "Not on your life or mine either."

I rescued my poster from the critics and buried it under my bed with "Uncle Sam"—steeple side down!

Hank found me observing the steeple of our church from my bed.

"Come on, Melanie. Take heart. When you get the words on your poster, everybody will know it's a church poster."

"No, they won't," I said. "Nobody understands me. It would take people as long to understand my poster as it would take me to stop 'drowning' when I speak in public."

"Drowning!" Hank exclaimed. "What do you mean by 'drowning' in public?"

I went on to tell Hank about the trials and tribulations I suffered just before I opened my mouth to speak in public.

Hank listened through to the end and then said, "You're making 'somebody' real happy when you let something that happened yesterday bog you down that way. Did you know that?"

"Well, it's not me that's happy over it, and I don't know who could be that mean."

"The old dickens himself, Melanie. He loves it when people feel guilty and bad—tickles him to death. He's in fat heaven over it all. He knows people can't do anything right when they're carrying a load of guilt around. He's having a ball right now, knowing he can make you feel bad and guilty just any old time he wants to."

"What? You mean God doesn't make people feel guilty? It's the devil who does?"

"That's right, Melanie. He wrote the book on it. Old Lucifer Dickens is the author of *guilt*. And you're pleasing him to death when you feel that way, so stop doing it! You hear?"

"Yes, I hear," I answered, still foggy over the new light that had just been turned on. I wondered how Hank could come up with all the answers he had for things, but it sure made more sense to me than anything had in a long time. What an awakening—like breathing fresh air again.

"And about that poster you made, Melanie. The Lord knows your good intentions, so don't worry about what other people think. Sometimes you do sweep the stars from the heavens maybe, but so what? Someday you're going to shine. Wonders never cease. You might even set the world on fire. I wouldn't be a bit surprised."

Sometimes Hank could believe twelve impossible dreams all in a day's thinking and all at the same time.

SEVENTEEN
Reverie Retreat

WITH the passing of spring came the closing of school. I was glad to have more time for dreaming and wishing and thinking on things. The summer nights were hot and nothing seemed to stir at times but the insects. Lillian and I sat on the front-porch steps and looked for the first evening star to wish upon.

"Stars look like little nuggets of shiny white gold, don't they?" Lillian said. "What do you think they look like, Melanie?"

"Oh, they make me think of street lamps on the floor of heaven, or of luminous flowers growing there just to make you and me want to go there and pick them."

"I wouldn't want to pick stars from the sky. Then people wouldn't have anything left to wish upon," Lillian said, matter-of-factly.

"No, they wouldn't, and people always

Looking for the first evening star

need at least one thing to hope for or one little dream to hold on to."

"I know," Lillian said. "See that corn patch across the road? It's Mr. Little's dream every spring, and it's starting to come up again. It's hard to believe that one cornstalk grows from only one tiny seed. It's fun to watch things grow from a seed—like watching your dreams come true. And they start with a tiny thought in your head—like a seed."

"But they have to be watered and fed like seeds, or they'll die. There's nothing sadder than a dream that has died," I said.

"I'll never let go of mine. I can't stand to see anything die."

Dan came to the screen door behind us. "It's 9:30, girls. Almost time to hit the hay."

"We're coming, Dan," I said. "Lil, would you believe me if I told you what I saw in that corn patch one morning?"

"Oh, yes." Lillian's eyes grew huge.

"It was early one morning, and I was standing in the front room there, and I heard a truck stop in front of Mr. Little's corn patch. The corn was seven feet tall at least. *The mailman is awfully early,* I thought, and I peeped out the window. Just as I did, the back doors of a white bread truck flew open. And guess what jumped out and took off through the corn field?"

"I don't know," Lillian said, anxiously. "Tell me."

"A convict, an *escaped* convict! And there was a chain still hanging from one of his arms! He had on a striped chain-gang suit with a little round hat to match, and . . . you don't believe me, do you, Lil? Nobody believes me, but I saw it. With my own two eyes I saw it."

"'Course I believe you, Melanie. I believe Jake when he tells me stories about real live hobos he sees waving to him from the boxcars on the railroad track with their clothes in a sack on the end of a pole. He's even talked to some hobos!"

"Come on. Let's get to bed," I said.

Nighttime was the best time to think about things. The night was made for dreaming anyway, and we had the stars to help us. Lillian and I listened to the sounds of night in our bunks after all the lights were out. The heavens were a wondrous sight from our bunk beds, and the moon peeped in to light our room just right. Crickets sang to each other nearby. The outline of the steeple rose higher above the world than anything I could see from my window. I could almost hear the steeple speaking to me sometimes. It pointed straight to the stars and gave me an awfully good feeling inside.

Over on the four-lane highway, the engines of the big transfer trucks hummed their way north and south. Somebody's dogs howled from deep in the holler. But the white ruffled curtains framing our opened window never moved to the sound of anything.

"Lil, honey, would you mind praying for a breeze?" I whispered toward the bunk above me.

"But, Melanie, I always do all the prayin', it seems. I always say grace. Everybody should start doing some prayin' of their own, now and then. Why don't you pray for a breeze, Melanie?"

"Ummm, OK," I yawned. "It's just that you're up there so much closer to heaven than I am down here. I thought God might hear you better."

"I'm no closer to heaven than you are, Melanie. God hears you same as he hears me."

I wondered at Lillian's words and fanned myself with the sheet. "Oh, it's too hot to pray or think or do anything, isn't it, Lil?"

"'Course not. It's hotter up here than it is down there, and it doesn't keep me from praying. You can pray silently if you don't want me to hear."

"All right, Lil."

I turned my pillow over to the cool side and moved my leg, searching for a cooler spot on the sheet. A fly buzzed around the room and lit on the window screen. I settled down to some of my own silent praying. "Dear Lord, please, . . . ouch!" I said, slapping at a mosquito which had just bit my arm.

"Shh, I was almost asleep," she said softly, "and you're going to wake up Elizabeth!"

"I'm sorry, honey. A mosquito bit me on the arm. Maybe we should pray for some rain clouds to cool things off, Lil."

"Not thunder clouds, though, Melanie, 'cause they scare me."

"No, not thunder clouds, but they're all the same. When I was your age, I thought clouds were giant cotton puffs which carried angels around heaven. Why you can't even sit down on one, much less play a harp on one. You can't even take a bite of one or hold a piece of cloud in your hand, 'cause they're nothing but vapors that leave you feeling rained on."

"You should believe that clouds are what you want 'em to be, Melanie. When kids at school try to tell me there isn't any Santa Claus, I never believe them, 'cause it wouldn't be Christmas without Santa Claus, and without Jesus, there wouldn't be Christmas!"

"Yeah, you're right, Lil. I should believe in what makes me happy since reality sometimes puts such a damper on things. From now on, clouds carry angels, instead of rain all the time."

"Melanie, when it thunders out, does that mean God is scolding his children for displeasing him?"

"Heavens, no! If that were the case, there'd be thunder twenty-four hours a day. It means the heavenly orchestra is warming up for a huge concert. They're getting their horns and harps all in tune— you know how bad orchestras sound tuning up. It sounds awful, but they have to do it, so everybody will play in harmony. Maybe it's to remind us down here to stay in tune for more harmony, too. Why don't you think of it that way, Lillian, so you won't be afraid anymore when thunderstorms come?"

"Oh, I've already started doing that. I'm not as afraid anymore, but I wonder if they'd let Jake practice with them sometime. That horn he brought home has never once played on tune."

"Oh, they'd probably let him," I said yawning, "but he'd have to practice out in the yard. Dan won't let him play that thing in this house anymore, since he played it for Miz Magnolia Blos—I mean Miz Alexandria, that day, and she's gone around with a hearing aid every since."

"Melanie, I think it's time we said those prayers, don't you?"

"Yes, I do, Lillian. Good night, honey."

I gave Lillian's bottom a little poke through the mattress with my toe. It always seemed to send her off to the faraway land of sleep.

My arm itched from the mosquito bite. I wasn't sleepy anymore. I could soon tell by Lillian's deep breathing that she was fast asleep. And nothing would disturb Elizabeth from her beauty sleep. I gently switched on the small lamp by the bed and eased open a drawer in the nightstand, where I found two books I could read: *Little Women* or one about Blackbeard. I chose the one on Blackbeard.

It was against the rules to burn a light in the house after ten o'clock. A light on anywhere in the house kept Dan awake. I could have been three flights up and behind a vaulted door with a light on, and

"You're wastin' 'lectricity. . . ."

that light would still bother Dan. No
sooner had the thought entered my mind
than I heard Dan hit the floor. I grabbed
Lillian's Bible from the nightstand, opened
it quickly, and slipped "Blackbeard" inside
it. Dan cracked the bedroom door and
peeped his head in.

"What're you doin', Melanie?" he asked.

"I—I'm reading the Bible," I said, quivering a bit.

"Well, what're you readin' that can't wait 'til tomorrow?"

"I—I'm reading about how you're supposed to let your light shine and not hide it under a bushel."

"Well, you'll have to let it shine tomorrow. The Lord made night for sleepin'. Now, turn the light off and go to sleep. You're wastin' 'lectricity."

I looked at the forty-watt bulb by my bed and smiled. "All right, Dan. Good night." I put the books away in the drawer and put out the light.

As far as I knew, there was only one place in the world that I could go where no one would bother me. That was Mr. Reavis' outhouse, but it had spiders in it, and I disliked spiders. Jake said that a black king snake lived behind it in the honeysuckle vines and would eat you alive. He'd swallow you whole and take a year to digest you. No wonder no one bothered you in the outhouse!

I hugged my pillow and said a prayer for Mama and several other important matters. Then I thought of the beautiful white dress I'd wished for earlier on the front porch when Lillian and I had seen the first evening star. I saw myself wearing it and running in slow motion across a meadow full of white daisies. On the other side of the daisy field, David Deyton stood waiting for me with outstretched arms.

EIGHTEEN
Choosing Up Careers

CHOWTIME was when family meetings were held. It was like taking two birds with one stone. Anything that saved time suited Dan just fine. Lillian and Jake sometimes approached Dan with all their wants and needs right at chowtime.

"If we can't have a tractor, then why can't we have a billy goat?" Jake asked one evening.

"Because I said so," Dan answered.

"Well, they don't smell as bad as you think," Jake said. "Mr. Reavis next door has goats. Even our cousins, Otis and Melvin, have goats. 'Course, they live in the country, but that makes no difference. *Everybody* has goats."

"Oh, no, they don't!" Dan said. If everybody ate mud pies, would you eat mud pies, too?"

"Well, no, but a goat would eat the grass."

"So you wouldn't have to mow it. Right?" Dan said.

"Right," Jake said through a mouthful of food.

"Don't talk with your mouth full!" Elizabeth said. "It makes me sick."

Dan crumbled a hunk of corn bread into a glass of sweet milk and took a bite with his soup spoon. "I'm not goin' to let you get lazy on me, Jake, so the billy goat is out. I don't want to hear any more about it. Now eat your supper."

Dan had no use for someone who was lazy, "lowdown triflin', and of plain no account." He continued, "Once a body gets lazy, he don't ever amount to anythin'."

"I'm going to amount to something," Hank announced. "Now, I know what I want to do in life, and I bet nobody can guess it."

"That's easy to guess," Elizabeth said. "You're going to be a preacher."

"Why do you say that?" Hank asked, smiling curiously.

"Because of the way you go to church meetings all the time and because of the way you go around singing hymns so much."

"Melanie goes to church every time I go. She's as curious as I am about what Mrs. Willis might come up with next," Hank said, turning in my direction. "Does that mean you're going to preach, Melanie?"

"Only to Jake," I said. "When he needs it."

"And it's my Waterloo, too, when she flies up at me like that," Jake said, gulping down another bite.

"Elizabeth, you can preach as well as anybody around here," Hank continued, "so I'll let you take over the job. Anyway, preaching to all of you is a sideline with me now. You'll have to guess again."

"Are you going to be a missionary?" Lillian asked. "That's what I want to be— a missionary or a veterinarian."

"No, I'm not going to be a missionary either, Lil. Guess again."

"A politician?" I asked.

It was here that Dan put the old "quietus" on our guessing game. "Ain't no brother a mine's goin' to be no crooked politician. I'd be hanged first. I'd ruther see him as a polecat."

"Grandpa Harris was a politician," I said. "The dyed-in-the-wool kind."

"Yeah, and he wern't crooked," Jake added. "Hank's the spittin' image a Grandpa, anyway. Talks your head off like Grandpa. Knows everythin' and everybody just like Grandpa. Why, Hank could get a sign pole to vote for him."

"Well, you're wrong again," Hank said. "I'm not going to be a politician."

"Whatcha gonna be then?" Jake asked.

"A pharmacist," Hank answered.

"Great day in the mornin'! What is that? A fancy word for *farmer?*" Jake exclaimed, nearly choking on his food.

"No, it's a professional person who fills doctors' prescriptions," Hank explained. "A druggist. You know. . . ."

Well, we shouldn't have been too surprised by Hank's revelation. After all, he'd gotten a job for the summer down at Pike's Drugstore as he'd planned.

"Awh, I wouldn't do that," Jake said. "Nobody can read a doctor's writin'. It looks like chicken scratch."

"That's because it's written in Latin," Hank said.

Dan spread his elbows out on the table and leaned way over his plate. Whenever Dan did that, we knew it was the signal to listen. It meant he was leaning over to say something important. He looked at Hank over the top of his glasses.

"If you've got to learn Latin, boy, and medicine and all, that means you got to go to college, don't it?"

For the first time in his life, Hank's three-hundred-watt smile began to dim. Hank cleared his throat and we all waited for his answer. "Yes, it does mean that, Dan."

"How you gonna do it?" Jake asked. "College costs money, and you know money don't grow on. . . ."

Dan put his hand out to silence Jake. "Hank knows whur money comes from," Dan said. "And any of you that don't know, well, it's time you learned. It comes from hard work. That's whur it comes from."

Dan turned to Hank again. "If that's what you want to do, boy, work hard. Then you can go to college. You can set the trail for the rest a this family to go, too—if they've a mind to," Dan said, nodding his head toward the rest of us.

"We can?" we asked in unison.

"Yep, you can. I ain't never had much education myself," Dan said, spooning his corn bread milk shake. "No more than just high school, and it's kinda late for me to start now. But it ain't too late for the rest a you. I'd like to see all a you get a college education. . . ."

Dan paused for another bite. "You know, one thing we ain't got is a whole lotta money. But if you've all a mind to go to college, I'll see you through—clear to the end."

"You'd do that for us?" Jake asked, astonished like the rest of us.

"Now, what did I say?" Dan asked back. "If you didn't hear me the first time, I ain't goin' to say it again."

Truer words had never been spoken, because if Dan hated one thing, it was having to tell you something twice. So, when he spoke, we listened well the first time. Dan never wasted anything— especially words.

"I heard you," Jake said. "I just couldn't believe what I heard—that's all."

"I heard you, too," Lillian cried, hopping off her chair to hug Dan's neck. "Oh, Dan, you're just right!" she beamed, squeezing him tight.

"But there's just one thing now," Dan said, trying to hold up under Lillian's love. "I don't want no educated fools around here, and I wanna know what it is you're goin' to do with it, once you get educated."

"There'll be stars in your crown, Dan, if you get all this bunch through college," Elizabeth said. Her eyes sparkled, as if she knew something we didn't.

"Well, I'll never have stars on my uniform," Dan said, frowning and grinning at the same time. "So I'll settle for stars in a crown, if that's what you say, Liz."

Even Dan was aware of Elizabeth's sixth sense. She just seemed to see things that no one else could see. Elizabeth never showed off her special gift of knowing, but when she said Dan would have stars in his crown, you can bet your bottom dollar, we counted on it.

"Why, Dan's five-star crown'll be so heavy that he won't even be able to wear it around heaven," Jake said. "He'll have to pull it in a wagon."

Dan didn't like being the center of attention for long, so he changed the subject. "Since Hank and Lillian know what they want to do someday, what about the rest of you?" Dan asked.

"Oh, I want to be a dress designer," Elizabeth gushed, "and have a dress shop all my own someday."

"What about you and Jake, Melanie?" Dan asked. "What're y'all gonna do?"

I never had to worry about answering to anything when I had Jake around to answer for me. "Uh, we don't know," Jake said, thoughtfully. "We'll have to think about ours, won't we, Melanie?"

"Oh, yes. Right. We will," I agreed, shaking my head.

Hank was so happy that he started singing another one of his favorite hymns, which happened to be at this eventful moment "Will There Be Any Stars in My

Crown?" He jumped up and started clearing off the table, and it wasn't even his turn to do dishes. We all knew Dan meant what he'd said again. He didn't fool around with words he didn't mean, especially when his horn-rims slid to the tip of his nose, and he wiggled his face into the frown that always kept them from falling off.

"Glory be! Hallelujah! I'm going to college!" Hank sang, as he flitted around the kitchen. "Let's all help with the dishes."

"Why don't you go light somewhere, Hank? You're fixin' to make me have a nervous breakdown," Jake said.

"Oh, I can't sit down now," Hank sang. "I got too much to do—too much to learn. I don't ever wanna sit down again!"

"I'd hafta sit down, if I had to learn Latin," Jake said. "Phwee—Latin. Can't you just see Hank someday, flyin' 'round a drugstore, waitin' on customers! Hank's Fly-By-Night Drugstore. . . . I can just hear him now. . . .

"'Why, yes, Ma'am, I'll take that subscription for you. Good grief, I can't read this. It looks like pig latin. . . . Why, it *is* pig latin! Take this back and tell that doctor I want it in real Latin. What do you think I went to college for? To learn *real* Latin! That's what for. Good, that's better.'

"'Now, let me see here. I'm sorry, Ma'am, we're all out of penicillin. Will aspirin do? 'Course aspirin's just as good. Take two, and call me in the mornin'. . . .'"

Dan laughed so hard he could hardly get down his last bite of corn bread milk shake. Watching Jake entertain us, we weren't getting much done on the dishes, either.

"That was really good, Jake! You do a good imitation of the best actor I know," Hank laughed. "Now let's see you imitate Lillian as a missionary veterinarian."

"Awh, heck. It'll be easy to imitate Lillian," Jake said. "Here's Dr. Lilly Q. Agnes's Animal Mission comin' to you from the worst side of Anytown, U.S.A. All strays—better known as 'sinners' to you—are welcome here."

Jake pranced toward the telephone, trying to walk like Lillian and singing "Bringin' in the Sheaves." He picked up the telephone receiver and started talking, "Yes, Ma'am, we take all animals at my mission. Most all we get are those sinner strays, though. . . . But I'll be glad to help your poor kitty. Calm yourself, Ma'am. Now, tell me your kitty's symptoms. . . . Uh, huh. Hmmm. . . . Now, we might have to operate. Sounds like she's got the dread disease. You say she's started eatin' ham bones and howlin' at the moon? Yes, your puddytat has all the symptoms, all right, of houndogitis. But we can cure it with a minor operation guaranteed to make your kitty purr again."

Jake hung up the telephone and took a bow, while all the dishpan hands applauded him. "Thank you," he said. "You'll be happy to know that Mrs. Smith down the street and her mother enjoyed it too. They had a conversation on the line when I picked up the phone. Three other people were listenin' in, so one fourth of the neighborhood heard me, too."

We all held our sides, laughing.

"Oh, Jake, surely you're jesting," Hank drawled. "What will all the neighbors say?"

"Nothin'," Jake answered. "I'm kiddin'. I knew nobody was on the phone." Jake pointed to the clock. "It's time for a train to go by."

Washing the dishes had never been so much fun. Dan didn't want to miss the show either, so he brought his army boots into the kitchen to polish them. You could always see your face in Dan's boots. He watched Jake's last performance at the same time. Dan didn't feel comfortable unless he was working on something.

"You've got to do one more before you stop, Jake," Hank said. "You can't leave out Madam Lizzy Lee and her fancy boutique, can you?"

"No, I reckon not, but aren't y'all finished with those dishes yet?"

"No," we said, unconcerned about the dishes. "Just once more, Jake, please?"

"Awh, all right," Jake said, "but I'll hafta go out and think about this one. It ain't gonna be easy to imitate Liz as a highfalootin' lady. I'll holler when I'm ready."

We washed dishes frantically during our

intermission, until Jake hollered, "OK, here I come as 'Lizzy Lee, the Thread Maker.' Y'all ready?"

"Yeah, we're ready!" we hollered back to Jake. Hank ran to the door and put his hands to his mouth like he was blowing Jake's horn, "Doot, doo doot, doo doot."

Jake outdid himself on his last act. It was almost more than we could stand. He strolled into the kitchen with a mop on his head. It hung down around his face like the hair of a rag doll. He flipped it away from his face and tossed his head back. Jake was wearing, of all things, one of my dresses with two pillowcases stuffed into the top of it. He looked pretty good, too.

Jake's tennis shoes stuck out from under my dress. Draped over one of his arms was the oldest dress Mama owned. It was the one she used to do her housework in, and it happened to be bright yellow. Jake held Mama's dress out as if he were trying to sell it to us.

"Madam," he said, looking at Hank, "this dress was made from *scratch,* just for you. Hmmf, of course, it's pure silk." Jake pranced around with his hand on his hip. "Pure *corn* silk. Grew it myself in flowerpots on my windowsill. Where else can you grow corn in Paris? Then my assistant here, Mrs. Webb, spun it into these beautiful golden threads for you. What do you mean, you don't trust my assistant? She's the best spinner in Paris. That spider makes more money than I do. No, it won't make you break out in a rash, but if it does, just put this grease on it.

Jake outdid himself on his last act. . . .

No, not on the dress—on your itch. It's my own secret potion. Not only will it keep you from itchin', it'll keep you from squeakin', and you can fry 'taters in it. It even makes your skin as smooth as silk— like this dress. Now, whad'ya say? A new dress and magic grease—what more do you want from corn?"

We all cried tears of laughter over Jake's grand finale. Elizabeth laughed so hard she had to borrow help from the kitchen sink to hold herself up.

"Ain't y'all finished with those dishes yet?" Jake asked, after his last bow.

"We're finished," I said, putting the last dish in the cabinet. "But it took all four of us as long to do the dishes, Jake, as it takes you to do them when you get stuck with extra KP alone."

"Phew, I timed that one perfect," Jake said, "but I was runnin' outta words."

NINETEEN
The Real Sally McQuarter

For nearly a week, I thought so hard about careers that my head ached. I narrowed them down to only a few, but it took Dan to put my feet on some solid, sensible ground. He brought me down to earth only after his temper got riled, but it forced some of the clutter from my head. Dan's patience was of short duration.

Dan stormed through the house, his voice more terrible than thunder. "All right, all right, I want everybody out here—*now*. That means *pronto*."

Everybody scrambled, pushing and shoving to stand at attention before Dan's wrath worsened.

"Where's Jake?" he demanded.

"I'm here," Jake said, stepping into his place and struggling to button his shirt, which was on wrong side out. He'd gone to church that way once, and we didn't notice it until we were home peeling potatoes.

"Well, you're one second late," Dan said, pointing to his watch. "Don't be late again."

Jake shook his head in total understanding. "I didn't have clothes on when you called us."

Sometimes Dan made ironclad statements just to keep us on our toes. Even though they seemed overbearing and too much to ask, they made us walk the line better.

"All right, now I want to know who choked the toothpaste to death, after I told y'all not to do it," Dan's voice rose higher and higher, "and who left the lid off the toothpaste, after I told y'all not to do it, and who didn't flush the commode, after I told y'all to *always* do it."

"Well, it wasn't me," Jake said.

"Me either," two voices chimed.

"It was me. I'm the one," I said. "I forgot. I was thinking about something—about something else—and forgot. I'm sorry."

"Detail, Melanie, detail. You'll never make it in this life without takin' care a detail. Now take care a that mess you left in the latrine. Don't be long about it either, and don't forget this time. Detail, you understand?"

"I understand," I said, making a beeline for the latrine.

Dan's voice trailed to his room. "How many times do I hafta say it? The word is *detail, detail, detail*."

I secured the bathroom door as well as I could—considering there wasn't a lock on

it—and gazed long at myself in the mirror.
I wrinkled my face into various expres-
sions to keep every emotion I owned
in good practice. It was also good practice
for the career I'd chosen. But the thought
of it created a frown of disappointment
which looked back at me from the mirror.
Dan would never accept the career I
wanted. Furthermore, he wouldn't stand for
it. I could never let him know the truth:
what I really wanted to be was a movie
star. He expected us to be sensible and
sane—as far as possible. He'd never know
how I dreamed of the footlights and a fan
club to adore me, and I would never have
to hear him say, "There will be no star-
struck, dizzy, blonde show girls in this
family!" Daddy would have said the same
thing, especially since he once stated that,
even if he could afford it, we still couldn't
take tap dancing or ballet lessons. He'd
never seen either tap dancers or ballerinas
wearing very many clothes!

I sighed into the mirror and turned
toward the window. There was the steeple,
pointing to heaven. I moved to the window
and propped my chin on the windowsill. If
only I could be inside the steeple at this
moment, with the birds way above all the
rooftops and chimneys and be closer to
heaven than from any other place in my
world.

A nun! I could be a nun and live in one
of those abbeys where all they do is
meditate. But then Jake wouldn't come to
see me in a nunnery. He'd have to leave
all his unacceptable noises, off-limit words,

203

and secret thoughts outside on the doorstep. Jake wouldn't feel right about forsaking his true self. And I couldn't do that to Jake. Besides, I even longed for a more colorful side myself.

No, I could never be a nun. Anyway, I'd have to change my religion and probably get a whole new identity because Baptists didn't have nuns in their churches.

I GI'd the latrine, as Dan had said, and brushed more of the clutter from my mind. I grabbed the first tube of paste I could find and squeezed some out on my toothbrush. I brushed my teeth vigorously, thinking what an awful-tasting paste that was. Then I looked at the tube with clear eyes. It was Brill Cream, Hank's latest hair discovery! Then and there, I decided that nothing happened by chance and that my most recent disaster could only mean one thing: I should be a hairdresser.

Dan went through the house, calling out, "All aboard. The tank is leavin' for town in two minutes flat. If you're goin' with me, you better come on, or you're goin' to get left."

The horn of Tin Lizzy Lee droned, "WHOO, WHOOOO." Sometimes it sounded more like a fog horn or one of those Mississippi riverboat horns I'd seen in the movies than a car which was taking off. One thing's for sure—it wasn't like any other car horn on this earth. I would have given a wooden nickel to know how that horn got on our car.

I raced out the door, just as Dan was

turning Tin Lizzy Lee around. Jake flung open the car door for me, and I stumbled onto the seat.

"One more minute, Mellie, and you'd a been left," Dan warned.

"I know," I said, remembering the one time that had actually happened.

Dan took us to the drugstore where Hank worked. Poor Jake's allergies were acting up, and we had to pick up some medicine for his runny nose. We all began piling into the drugstore and made a lot of noise until Dan told us, "Pipe down!"

Hank headed me off at the front door. "Guess who came in the store today?" he whispered through one corner of his mouth.

"David Deyton," I guessed, with big eyes.

"No," Hank said, disgusted.

"Well, then, who?"

"Miz Alexandria. She's back from her summer vacation in Vermont or wherever she goes. I couldn't avoid her. She followed me all around the store, asking me questions, but I'm running out of excuses, I tell you. She wanted to know what the holdup was with Mama coming home."

"Mercy sakes, what did you tell her, Hank? She probably thinks by now that we drove our poor mother crazy and that she's never coming home again."

"I told her that the engine exploded on our car. Then when we finally got it fixed to bring Mama home, Mama came down with a cold, and it turned into the 'oletimey consumption,' so her doctor wouldn't let her leave the hospital until she was all well again."

"Did Miz Got R—I mean, Miz Alexandria—believe all that?" I asked.

"Of course, she believed me."

"She'll pass the word around, you know, but since she believes you can walk on water and that what you say is the gospel, she won't know she's fibbing. Don't worry about it, Hank."

"Yeah, maybe you're right. I'll just have to tell her the very next time she asks— even if it does shiver her timbers a bit. And, Melanie, I still believe that we'll bring Mama home with us when we visit her again in two weeks."

"Hank, every time we've gone to visit Mama, you've believed that she'd be coming home with us when we left. One of these times, your honest believing is going to work, Hank! Maybe it will work two weeks from now."

"I think Mama is well enough to come home, but I'm not the doctor. Even Elizabeth hasn't tried to play doctor. She hasn't said a word about what she thinks."

"I know, Hank. I've wondered what Elizabeth has been feeling in her bones, too. She keeps us all in suspense sometimes, and I think she does it on purpose."

"No, she doesn't. She just doesn't always tell what she's feeling. I wish Jake knew things like she does. He'd tell it all the minute he got the message, but maybe

Elizabeth doesn't get messages on everything. Maybe she just listens better and pays more attention, or could it be that she's some kind of genius? What're you wearing, Mel?" Hank asked, sniffing. "Are you wearing my Brill Cream?"

Just then, Lillian ran up, bumping her head on my hipbone. She grabbed her forehead and frowned painfully. "Oh, Melanie, you have sharp points!"

Lillian recovered and told us about a discovery she'd made. She'd run across the bargain table, and the items on sale were miracle hair remedies. She had spotted a home permanent which promised her endless curls and a new spring to her life. "It's just what I need, Melanie," she beamed. "Elizabeth read what the box said!"

Her only complaint in life was that her hair was as straight as a stick. She hated it because Jake said she looked like a Dutch boy with a salad-bowl haircut. Lillian also resented her round, little nose and round, little cheeks which matched all her other round, little features. She led me and Hank to the bargain table as though she'd uncovered a gold mine.

I found a box that claimed to transform me into a dazzling, subtle blonde if only I'd buy it. It said: *Tone down the gold in your hair. Be a more sophisticated blonde. Brighten up with Lusterblu.* I saw myself with hair like an angel's. I agreed with the box that its contents would do me good, so I snatched it up as though it were my last chance. Hank waited by the table for me and Lillian. He found some stuff for ten cents that guaranteed to make his bushel of waves as straight as an arrow. The yearning for change had taken hold of Hank, Lillian, and me. We couldn't wait to see our new images. Elizabeth told us we'd live to regret it, but we didn't hear a word she said.

"I wouldn't put that stuff on my head. You've all gone mad," Elizabeth scoffed. "You're ignoramuses! That's what you are. Oh, well, go ahead. Nobody listened to Noah either—and they all drowned."

The next morning the three "change-thirsty nincompoops," as Elizabeth labeled us, set out on our beautification adventure.

While the gook was taking its toll on my head, I rolled Lillian's silky brown hair on skinny little rods. *My career has only begun,* I mused. Hank madly indulged his head in the whole jar of hair straightener. We each allowed ourselves forty-five minutes for the wonder-working potions to rearrange our looks. Then we took turns at the sink, washing it all off.

Hank took over the mirror in the bathroom while Lillian and I tiptoed toward our room. We planned to surprise everybody. We peeked around for Jake and Elizabeth. They were in the dining room, deeply involved in a game of Monopoly and at each other's throats for the best property deeds.

"If you won't sell Park Place, I'll swap you three deeds for it," Jake said.

"What are you going to swap me?" Elizabeth asked suspiciously.

"How about Baltic and Mediterranean Avenues, plus Electric Company?"

"Ha!" Elizabeth bolted. "Electric Company sounds reasonable, but I wouldn't give ten cents for those other two deeds. You cheapskate."

"OK, how about all three deeds, plus my Get-out-of-Jail-Free card?"

"No," Elizabeth said flatly.

"Well, how about all that I've promised so far? And to top it off, I'll go to jail for my next five turns."

"That's just where you should be, Jake, you know that—in jail. This game makes you turn crooked, but I'm not selling out to you, and that's final!" Elizabeth said, stomping her foot.

Jake was determined to outlast Elizabeth until doomsday. Around they went like a circle saw while Lillian and I sneaked safely by them and vanished into our room.

I unwrapped the towel from around my head. Lillian suddenly grew wide-eyed and pale. "What's wrong?" I asked. "I only took the turban off my head."

"Mel—Melanie," she stammered. "Your hair looks awfully dark."

"Nonsense!" I retorted. "It just looks that way 'cause it's wet. It'll dry a lot lighter. You'll see. Now, don't look so sick about it. When Hank gets done with the bathroom mirror, we'll both be able to see our new selves."

"Oh, I don't know if I want to see my new self, since I've seen yours," she said, frowning sickly.

Around they went like a circle saw. . . .

It was hard to see in the mirror over our
dresser, thanks to the way the light hit it.

"Now, don't go by that mirror, Lil. It
never shows you up right. You know that.
We can tell how we *really* look by the
bathroom mirror. Now fluff your hair so it
will dry well."

We combed and fluffed, combed and
fluffed. The dryer Lillian's hair became,

210

the more it bushed out into kinky strands. It began to resemble a porcupine—one that had been struck by lightning.

I panicked inside but tried not to alarm her. Lillian was speechless. "Now, honey, a haircut will calm your hair down a lot," I said reassuringly.

"But I don't want my hair cut, Melanie."

Fretting over hers, I'd forgotten about my own hair. By the time hers had dried, neither of us could get a comb through it. Hank walked into our room. His mouth fell open, but he quickly collected his composure, when he saw our reaction to his own change in appearance.

"Hank," I said, pointing to his topknot. "It's flat. Your hair is flat and greasy, except for those little, wild hairs springing up here and there, but it's never been flat before."

"Oh, yeah? Well, you ought to see yours, Melanie. It's blue—navy blue. Did you know that, Melanie?" Hank asked.

I leaned over close to the bedroom mirror and prayed that it was deceiving me. I ran to look in the bathroom mirror. It was true. The other mirror I'd distrusted hadn't lied at all. My hair *was* navy blue. The tears swelled in my eyes and ran down my cheeks.

"Merciful heaven. Dear Lord in heaven. Oh, Lord, have mercy," I cried over and over.

"Now, Melanie, don't be so upset. It'll all come out in the wash eventually," Hank said, cheerfully.

"No, it won't!" I sobbed. "Oh, Hank,

It was
true. . . .
My hair
was
navy
blue.

we're all ruined for life. What are we going to do?"

"I'm going to start a new trend with my new image. I know it looks like I dumped all the grease in Grandma's lard bucket on my head, but so what? I'll just say I got my head stuck in it by accident. After a while, everybody will go hang his head in a lard bucket. That's how trends get started," Hank said laughing.

I groaned out a flood of tears.

"How can you laugh? Elizabeth's right. We've all gone mad. Dan and Liz are the only sane children Mama has. I just want to die!"

"Now, Melanie, look at it this way," Hank reasoned. "What difference will it make twenty years from now? It's neither here nor there."

"It is here and now!" I insisted. "Ju—ju—Just look at us. We're all wrecked. Lillian looks like I plugged her into an electrical socket. You look like a red-neck greaser, and I've turned into a solid blue batik. It's not a bit humorous. We're marked for life."

"Don't forget that Jake was an onion head for two weeks, but he's recovered. Maybe blue hair isn't all that bad. What if it were army green? We don't look all that deplorable," Hank remarked. "There's no use crying over spilled milk. Just wash your hair a couple more times and you'll look like your old self again—someday. Then it'll be water under the bridge."

By this time, Lillian was coming out of her shock—a little, anyway. "The fairies

say that you should never cry over spilt
milk, because whenever milk is spilt,
somebody, somewhere, comes out to the
better."

Hank agreed with her wholeheartedly.
That made me insist, "Whooom, for
goodness sake—I'd just like to know?"

"Whooom?" Hank repeated.

"Yes, just 'whooom' is coming out to the
better on this since we are all clearly
ruined for life? Now, just tell me, Hank,
'who' is it?"

"Mr. Pike," Hank said, not minding
having to eat humble pie. "We bought his
hair remedies that nobody else wanted."

I washed my hair around twenty or
thirty times until it faded from navy blue
to silver. Hank said I should roll it all up
in big silver curlers and claim I was the
latest model of a spaceship. He also spent
some time over the washbasin, trying to
force some of the grease from his head
down the drain. A haircut from me calmed
Lillian's frizz into soft ringlets around her
face, but I feared I'd have to cut my whole
head off before I'd see the golden-haired
girl appear in my mirror again. I decided
that the whole experience had ended my
career as a hairdresser even before it had
gotten started.

Finally Jake, Lillian, Hank, and I
sufficiently resembled our old selves so
that Mama would not go into intensive
care when she saw us again. All I could
think of was how our shenanigans would
be the death of Mama if she ever found
out what we'd done to our hard heads.

Dan was put out enough with us, and Elizabeth said only once, "I told you so." Jake said Elizabeth was right about the whole lot of us, that we were all "genuwine knuckle-headed, ignoramus nincompoops!"

Jake and Lillian both spared no feelings in calling it "like they saw it." Perhaps that shows that children are the most honest and sometimes the wisest of all people.

The day before we were to visit Mama again, Dan announced, "Sally McQuarter is comin' to supper here tonight, and I want this house GI'd from top to bottom."

"The real Sally McQuarter?" Jake asked. "I didn't think there really was one."

"Well, there is," Dan assured us. "And you're all gonna meet her tonight, 'cause I'm bringin' her here to this house. You know what I'll expect. This house'd better be in top-notch condition when I come home. And make yourselves presentable, too. Understand?"

"We understand," we said in unison.

"Good. Now I'm goin' to get Tin Lizzy Lee worked on so it don't fall apart on the way to the hospital tomorrow. Remember, spic-and-span, and don't overlook a thing."

Dan marched to the car as if he were going to pick up the President at the White House.

"Dan's worked on that car all week," Hank said. "I don't understand why somebody has to spend another whole day with her!"

"You'll see," Elizabeth said.

"Maybe he's getting her painted, huh, Liz? All the girls I dated didn't mind riding in her when she was rusty. The real Sally McQuarter must really be something. You know, this'll be the first time Dan's ever brought a girl home."

"Oh, I bet she ain't no prettier 'n Liz," Jake said. "Why, I wouldn't be surprised if she's cross-eyed and has buck teeth." Jake's facial contortions reinforced his description of the supposed Sally.

"Thanks a lot, Jake, for the compliments," Elizabeth retorted.

"I was talking about Liz, the *car*," Jake said.

"OK, let's get down to brass," Hank ordered. "You know I'm in charge when Dan's not around."

We cleaned every nook and cranny of the house. We washed and waxed the floors, then scrubbed down the latrine. Not a single detail was overlooked. The house sparkled. We looked like five polished cadets ourselves. If only Mama could see us now! She'd be proud of Dan's homemade army.

Hank arranged seven roses in an empty honey jar since someone had knocked down our only vase with a basketball! We planned to take them the next day to Mama at the hospital. We'd finally collected enough pennies to buy her something nice—a rose from each child and a special one for her. Hank said Mama wouldn't mind if Sally saw them before she did. After all, it wasn't every day that the real Sally McQuarter came to supper, so we all agreed.

While we waited for Dan and his mystery guest, Hank briefed us on manners. "Now don't show all your colors at once. Be polite, and no whooping and hollering. Say 'Yes, Ma'am' and 'No, Ma'am.' Try not to say *ain't* if you can help it, Jake. Lord help us. Act civilized— not like heathens, morons, and . . . ."

"There's a car turning in," Elizabeth said, looking straight at all of us.

The green tank flashed by the window. Jake ran to look with the rest of us behind him. The mystery of Sally McQuarter was too much to bear.

"Does he have Sally with him?"

"I think so."

"Did you see her?"

"What does she look like?"

"Well, who got a look at her?"

Jake raised a hand in the air, then pointed to himself. His other hand was holding his heart while he started falling all around, making believe he was having a heart attack. He fell on the couch, stretching himself out like a corpse. "I got a look at her," he said, "and—and if Sally doesn't look like I believe she does, I'll eat those roses over there."

"Oh, heavens, Jake, what does she look like?" We gasped. "We can take it. Tell us."

"I bleeve," Jake said, planting his eyes heavenward, "that Sally's a girl like Mama."

Polished cadets

Jake was right about the real Sally McQuarter. It was Mama after almost a year away from us, and her homecoming was a reunion as you've never seen before. I wish you could have been there, too.

Twenty years have passed since this story happened, and Dan's still as American as apple pie and dumplings. He's in his forties, and wears his army uniform to work everyday. It has five stars on it now, but only rare eyes can see them. They're there as bright and shining as morning stars. If you don't believe me, ask the five who put them there: Hank, Elizabeth, Jake, Lillian, and me, Melanie.

Epilogue

You might be interested to know what happened to Mama and all those children you read about. Beginning with the oldest to the youngest child, we are:

Dan, *who is now a warrant officer in the United States Army Reserves. He has never married, and still lives at home with Mama. His most heroic deeds were done on the home front—right at his doorstep. He kept his promise to us children. Those who wanted to continue their education beyond high school went to the college of their choice—with Dan's blessings and full support.*

Hank, *who graduated from the University of South Carolina School of Pharmacy with an award for outstanding achievements made during his years there. He is now a commander in the United States Navy and is chief pharmacist at the*

Annapolis Naval Academy. Hank is also a championship skipper. He is married and has three children.

Melanie, who graduated from East Carolina University in Greenville, North Carolina, with a degree in interior design and elementary art education. She is a former elementary art teacher, and had a small arts-and-crafts shop for five years before she began writing and illustrating children's books. She lives in Harrisburg, North Carolina, with her husband and son.

Elizabeth, who graduated from Florida State University with a degree in fashion retailing and home economics. She is a buyer of women's apparel for a chain of seventeen large department stores, and lives in St. Petersburg, Florida, with her husband and daughter.

Jake, who graduated from high school but did not choose to attend college. He became a professional house painter and has remained a bachelor. Jake still lives at home with Dan and helps take care of Mama.

Lillian, who attended Newberry College in South Carolina for two years. She has resumed her studies presently at Armstrong College in Savannah, Georgia. Her husband is a football coach and math instructor at a private Christian school. Lillian is also an historic tour guide. She and her husband have two sons.

Finally, there is Mama who still lives in the same saltbox house we all grew up in. She is now in her sixties and has been in perfect health since the time of this story until recently when we learned that she is gradually losing her eyesight. Nevertheless, her joyful spirit and faith remain a constant inspiration to her children and grandchildren.

We are still having family get-togethers like the ones you read about in the book. And everybody still gets "hugged from the knees up" since some of us now have little ones who run around just as Lillian did in the story.

If you're ever in the Blue Ridge Mountains of North Carolina on the hottest day in August and think that you hear the echoes of children's laughter somewhere in the distance, it could just be us. We go to the hills to feed our souls. The family gourmets take care of our stomachs.

You'll probably find us at the highest altitude, where air conditioning comes straight from heaven and where rhododendron and mountain laurel practically pour into the windows that open like big glass doors. We'll be roughing it probably in a huge rustic cabin with two balconies and rows of green rocking chairs filled with lots of people. Someone may be holding a baby on a bouncing knee. You'll also meet other family members, especially the ones "who know more tales about the Rainbow Army Gang than anybody and still love them at least one-and-a-half times more than anybody else."

You'll recognize us by the noise, a few little green army tents (compliments of a favorite uncle—Dan) pitched here and there for our children to camp out in, and a long, shiny green car, also Uncle Dan's. You might notice a large white naval sail draped like a tent across the upper balcony deck. That's for any brave little campers who get "spooked in the night" from too many North Carolina ghost tales or get cold and decide to break camp for cozier "tent" quarters on the balcony.

In the evening you'll hear a loud bugle sounding taps. The morning will bring reveille, along with the song, "Nothing Could Be Finer than to Be in Carolina in the Morning." Sometimes you may see feathers flying from a harmless pillow fight, probably instigated by another favorite uncle—Jake, who is still the biggest kid of all. (You might smell chicken, though, nicely barbecuing on Hank's famous grill.)

It'll be the bright, colorful flag streamers strung across both balconies by Hank, which will convince you that you've found a band of gypsies. "When a naval commander is in port," says Hank, "he *always* puts out his flags," which in this case mean "Welcome" and "Beware—for he who comes here could be hugged from the knees up!"

THE END